The Pocket Essential

# The Slayer Files

**A completely and utterly unauthorised guide to BUFFY THE VAMPIRE SLAYER**

www.pocketessentials.com

First published in Great Britain by Pocket Essentials, 18 Coleswood Rd, Harpenden, Herts, AL5 1EQ, England, 1999.

Distributed in the U.S.A. by Trafalgar Square Publishing, P.O.Box 257, Howe Hill Rd, North Pomfret, Vermont 05053



Series Editor: Paul Duncan



A CIP catalogue record for this book is available from the British Library.

ISBN 1903047 02 1

9 8 7 6 5 4 3 2 1

Book typeset & cover designed by DP Fact & Fiction.

Printed and bound by Cox & Wyman

*for Crow, Topper and Lilith who put up with my general lack of any sense at all—I love you*

## Welcome to Buffyville!

Sixteen-year-old Buffy Summers moves to Sunnydale from LA with her mother, Joyce, hoping to leave her troubled past behind. Fat chance. Almost immediately Principal Bob Flutie tell her he won't hold the fact that she burned a gymnasium down at her previous school against her (the climactic event of Joss Whedon's original script for the *Buffy* movie). And five minutes later the Librarian announces he's her Watcher and she's the Slayer...

### How did we get here?

Riding high in 1996 as the scriptwriter of *Toy Story,* Joss Whedon must have had mixed feeling about revisiting the scene of his 1992 movie *Buffy The Vampire Slayer.* Not only had the movie, partly intended to launch the movie career of Luke Perry (*Beverley Hills 90201*), been a flop, but director/producer Fran Rubel Kuzui had mocked Whedon's original script in the press, citing its humour and martial arts action as one of the reasons it had been heavily re-written. So why was Whedon ready to team up with Kuzui again to launch *Buffy* as a TV show for Warner Brothers 1997 season?

It's difficult to find anyone with a bad word for Whedon, and he's certainly never dissed Kuzui publicly, so maybe he's a nice guy, or maybe he wanted to fulfil his original vision for Buffy, but thank God he did. Because with *Welcome To The Hellmouth,* on the 10th of March 1997 we were introduced to the dark, funny and downright scary world of *Buffy the Vampire Slayer,* Whedon style.

In these days of success for Sarah Michelle Gellar (the world's sexiest woman according to *FHM* magazine) those not in the know place the reason for *Buffy*'s success at her feet. Those who watch the show know differently—Buffy is, above everything else an ensemble show, as if *Friends* had wandered into *The X-Files.* Despite the show's tendency to remake every monster movie genre going, it's always the interaction of the cast that stands out, rather as the genuine warmth and characterisation of Stephen King's writing marks him out from others in the horror genre.

## Buffy

In the Buffy movie we learn about Slayers, and we get a reminder every week: *"In every generation there is a Chosen One. She alone will stand against the vampires, the demons and the forces of darkness. She is the Slayer."* As we know that vampires are the revenants of the demons that walked the earth, we presume that the forces of good have created Slayers, all of them being nubile young girls so far (will a boy slayer ever emerge?).

Sarah Michelle Gellar, whose comeliness, wit and grace have formed our picture of Buffy, was originally cast for the part of Cordelia. Whew, that was a close one. She started her acting career in commercials and prior to *Buffy* was modelling fashions on *Regis and Kathy Lee.* Since *Buffy* she has starred in both horror —*Scream 2*—and the black comedy *Cruel Intentions,* proving herself to be seriously good at this acting business.

## Xander Harris

Alexander (Xander) LaVelle Harris, the Chandler Byng (if you don't know, look it up) of *Buffy,* was born and raised in Sunnydale (how did he survive so long?), and has known Willow since childhood. Jesse (dead in *The Harvest*) was Xander's other friend, until Xander accidentally staked him. In Buffy he's a wild card emotionally, but is incredibly brave (or very stupid), and has pulled the fat from the fire on nearly as many occasions as he's thrown it in. He's not going to university, and it's unknown what he'll be doing next season.

Nicholas Brendon (born April 12, 1971) lost his original goal (to play professional baseball) when he broke his arm. Before *Buffy* his first job was a Clearasil commercial followed by a stint on *Dave's World.* Nicholas lives with his identical twin brother, Kelly, who is often mistaken for Nick. Well duh!

## Willow

Willow Rosenberg, another Sunnydale native, was born to Ira and Sheila Rosenberg. Her mother seems to be a ditz of Joyce Summers proportions. Willow dated Xander briefly when they were five, until he stole her Barbie doll. She quickly became best friends with Buffy Summers. Willow is a computer nerd with a happy ability to find exactly what is needed on the Web, while the rest of us are still cursing our computers. After Jenny Calendar's demise she has taught computer class and has inherited Jenny's interest in paganism and the occult and has successfully performed a few spells. Next season Willow plans to continue her exploration of witchcraft while attending UC Sunnydale.

Alyson Lee Hannigan, (born March 24, 1974), has been in show business since the age of four, modelling and appearing in commercials; McDonald's, Six Flags Amusement Parks, and Oreo cookies. She got her first big role, in the film *My Stepmother is an Alien* with Seth Green (Oz) playing her love interest. At the moment she is in *American Pie* (Paul Weitz, 1999), which is *very* rude, and is reportedly dating Marilyn Manson's drummer, so obviously doesn't share Willow's goody-two-shoes image.

### Rupert Giles

Rupert Giles is English and was born into a family of Watchers, attended Oxford University, where he dropped out for a while, dabbling in the occult and gaining the nickname Ripper. He returned to his destiny and worked as a museum curator in England until assigned to Buffy Summers. Like many real Brits his reserve, when pierced, can disappear, showing the nature of a race who won two world wars. That is to say he can be unexpectedly violent and completely over the top. It is unknown what he will be doing in season four, due to his place of employment no longer existing...

Anthony Stewart Head, (born February 20, 1954) comes from Hampton, England and is the son of documentary filmmaker Seafield Head and actress Helen Shingler. He's played Jesus in *Godspell* and Frank N Furter in *The Rocky Horror Show,* but prior to Buffy was sadly best known for his Nescafé Gold Blend (Taster's Choice in the US), ads in which he took an inordinate amount of time to get a date with his female neighbour.

### Angel

Angel is around 243 years old, born in Ireland in 1755 or 1756, and liked a drink—which is what led him into the arms of Darla thus creating Angelus (in the book I've distinguished between Angel and Angelus—they are played as different characters by Boreanaz) around 1780ish. He killed Drusilla's family and drove her mad, turning her into a vampire in 1860. In 1898 he was cursed by a Romany tribe, restoring his soul, and suffered guilt for the evil he'd done.

We next see him in New York city in the 1990s as Whistler a good demon (?), offers him redemption if he helps the Slayer—not only does he help her, he falls in love with her. The rest of the story is in this book. David Boreanaz (born May 16, 1971) who plays Angel worked parking cars and painting houses. Distinguished (if that's the right word) by a *Married With Children* episode, he was seen from a window by an agent while walking his dog, Bertha Blue. The agent called casting director Marcia Schulman and told her he'd found Angel. Obviously he had. David Boreanaz is starring in *Angel*, a spin off from *Buffy* starring along with Charisma Carpenter (they'll be written out of *Buffy*) Whedon says the show will be darker, more adult, and *"more of an anthology show"* than *Buffy*. Angel will leave Sunnydale to *"help tormented souls battle their personal demons in the grittier Los Angeles."* Cordelia goes to LA to pursue fame and fortune, and ends up working at a detective agency. Whether Angel and Cordelia will become romantically involved, Whedon says, *"We don't have that in the works."* There will be crossovers, but possibly only with characters like Spike.

*Angel* will debut on Warner Brothers in the fall of 1999; after Buffy, Tuesdays at 9:00 p.m. in the USA. God knows when it will turn up here—rumour hath it that Sky have picked it up. Perhaps next year you'll be buying an Angel Guide ... Please God!

### Cordelia Chase

Cordelia Chase, born and raised in Sunnydale, is an appealingly forthright snob, with a gift for saying the wrong thing at the wrong time. A relationship with Xander Harris dropped her credibility to zero with her cool friends. Events in series three will lead to her being offski to LA, just in time to catch up with *Angel*...

Charisma Carpenter, (born July 23, 1970) was born and lived in Las Vegas until she was fifteen, and after high school, she spent some time in Europe. She's had more jobs than the author (hitherto thought to be impossible); waitress, video store clerk, aerobics instructor, property manager and a San Diego Chargers Cheerleader. She's appeared in numerous commercials and was spotted by Aaron Spelling in a guest spot on *Baywatch* saw her, and was cast her as bitchy Ashley Green in *Malibu Shores*. She auditioned for the role of Buffy but also read for Cordelia—and a good job too.

## Oz

Oz doesn't seem to possess a last name and is quiet with a droll sense of humour. He is the guitarist for the band *Dingoes Ate My Baby* who seem to get a lot of work in Sunnydale. Oz was bitten by his cousin Jordy—a werewolf. No word on any afflictions born by the rest of his family, but his Aunt didn't seem surprised when he called her about it. We've seen Oz do the werewolf thing, and Willow's cool with it. Crazy guy! Who knows what Oz will be doing next season?

Seth Green's (born February 8, 1974) parents are Herbert, a maths teacher, and Barbara, an artist. Another commercial star, we can only look forward to someone producing a video of the cast of Buffy as they were... Froot Loops, Jello Pudding Pops, you get the picture, even co-starring with Sarah Michelle Gellar, when she was four years old. Seth was in the *Buffy* movie but the only evidence is a still on the back of the video box—his part was cut, which must leave him with mixed feelings. He's currently also famous as the disturbed son of Doctor Evil in the *Austin Powers* films and the snap-happy loon in the Kodak Gold advertisements.

## Spike

Spike is a joy to behold. After the first series melodrama of the Master (respect is due) Spike and Dru were a breath of fresh air. Calling the Anointed One the Annoying One, immolating him in the first episode he appears in and deciding to just not bother waiting for the Night of St Vigeous to kill Buffy, he's an antidote to the mystic seriousness that occasionally infects Buffy. And is loved in the UK *just* for not having a stupid cockerney accent. Spike (known as William the Bloody in previous times) was bitten by Drusilla in the 1800's, and was mates with Angel, killing two slayers. Arriving in

Sunnydale, in 1997 he left quickish when things went pear shaped, but returned when Drusilla cheated on him with a chaos demon. Thank the lord he's rumoured to be back in both *Buffy* and *Angel* this year.

James Marsters (born August 21 1971) is a native of Modesto, California, and paints, plays his guitar, and works on his Suzuki Samurai. Bleaching his hair hurts like hell, apparently, and the Brit accent is fake, but is coached by Anthony Stewart Head. He's mostly worked in the theatre in such plays as *Troilus and Cressida, Twelfth Night* and *Camino Real,* but he's guest starred on *Millennium* and *Northern Exposure,* among other TV shows. He's recently co-written a Spike and Drusilla comic for Dark Horse.

Spike: *"Now that was fun. Oh, don't tell me that wasn't fun. God, it's been so long since I've had a decent spot of violence."*

# Season One

## Regular Cast

Sarah Michelle Gellar (Buffy Summers), Nicholas Brendon (Xander Harris), Alyson Hannigan (Willow Rosenberg), Charisma Carpenter (Cordelia Chase), Anthony Stewart Head (Rupert Giles).

## Production Staff Credits

Executive Producer: Joss Whedon , Co-Producer: David Solomon, Producer: Gareth Davies, Executive Producers: Sandy Gallin; Gail Berman; Fran Rubel Kuzui; Kaz Kuzui, Co-Executive Producer: David Greenwalt , Story Editors: Matt Kiene & Joe Reinkemeyer; Rob Des Hotel & Dean Batali, Unit Production Manager/Co-Producer: Joseph M. Ellis, First Assistant Director: David D'Ovidio (4V01, 4V03, 4V05, 4V07); Brenda Kalosh (all even-numbered episodes); Ken Collins (4V09, 4V11), Second Assistant Director: Mark Hansson, Score: Walter Murphy, Theme: Nerf Herder, Director of Photography: Michael Gershman, Production Designer: Steve Hardie, Editor: Geoffrey Rowland (4V01, 4V04, 4V07, 4V10); Skip Schoolnik, A.C.E. (4V02); Regis B. Kimble (4V03, 4V06, 4V09, 4V12); Skip MacDonald (4V05, 4V08, 4V11), Casting: Marcia Shulman, C.S.A., Costume Designer: Susanna Puisto, Costume Associate: J.B. Annegan (4V03 only), Art Director: Carey Meyer, Set Decorator: David Koneff, Leadman: Gustav Gustafson, Construction Coordinator: Daniel Turk, Property Master Ken Wilson, Chief Lighting Technician: Larry Kaster, Key Grip: Tom Keefer, Camera Operator: Russ McElhatton, Script Supervisor: Lesley King, Script Coordinator: Amy Wolfram (4V03 only), Production Sound Mixer: David Kirschner, Post Production Coordinator: Jahmani Perry (4V01-4V05); Brian Wankum (4V07-4V12), Assistant Editor: Skip MacDonald (4V01, 4V03); Golda Savage (all even-numbered episodes); Kristopher Lease (4V05, 4V07, 4V09, 4V11), Post Production Sound: TODD AO STUDIO, Supervising Sound Editor: Ingeborg Larsen (4V01-4V06); Cindy Rabideau (4V07-4V12), Re-Recording Mixers: Kevin Patrick Burns; Jon Taylor; Todd Keith Orr, Music Editor: Celia Weiner, Production Coordinator: Susan Ellis, Assistant Production Coordinator: Claudia Alves, Production Auditor: Edwin L. Perez, Assistant to Joss Whedon: George Snyder, Assistant to David Greenwalt: Robert Price, Assistant to Gareth Davies: Marc D. Alpert, Stunt Coordinator: Jeff Smolek, Transportation Coordinator: Robert Ellis, Location Manager: Jordana Kronen, Costume Supervisor: Rita Salazar, Make-Up Artist: Todd McIntosh, Hair Stylist: Jeri Baker, Special Make-Up Effects: John Vulich; Optic Nerve Studios, Visual Effects: Area 51, Visual Effects Supervisor: Glenn Campbell, Supervising Animator: Scott Wheeler, Main Title Design: Montgomery/Cobb, Processing: 4MC, Post Production Services: Digital Magic.

## Season 1 Episodes

### Welcome To The Hellmouth (03/10/97), Episode:4V01

Written by Joss Whedon, Directed by Charles Martin Smith. (In the UK this was shown edited together with episode two, *The Harvest*, to make a single pilot film.)

...Sunnydale High School at night. A fist punches through a windowpane and reaches in to undo the clasp. A boy and a girl, Darla, are breaking into the school.

Darla: *"Are you sure this is a good idea?"*

Boy: *"It's a great idea, now come on."*

They crawl in. They leave the classroom and walk down the hall.

Darla: *"Do you go to school here?"*

Boy: *"I used to. On top of the gym it's so cool. You can see the whole town."*

She stops him.

Darla: *"I don't wanna go up there."*

Boy: *"You can't wait, huh?"*

Darla: *"We're just gonna get in trouble."*

Boy: *"Yeah, you can count on it."*

They almost kiss when Darla, startled, turns her head around to look down the hall.

Darla: *"What was that?"*

Boy: *"What was what?"*

Darla: *"I heard a noise."'*

Boy: *"It's nothing!"*

Darla: *"Uh, uh, maybe it's something."*

Boy: *"Or maybe it's some THING!"*

Darla: *"That's not funny."*

He looks down the other hall.

Boy: *"Hellooooo! There's nobody here."*

Darla: *"Are you sure?"*

Boy: *"Yes, I'm sure."*

Darla: *"Okay."*

She turns back to him, her face contorted into the predatory mask of a vampire. She snarls as she rips into his throat...

...and we are in the world of Buffy Summers.

On her first day at Sunnydale High School Buffy soon makes friends with Xander Harris (Sunnydale High's answer to Chandler Byng) and computer nerd Willow Rosenberg, costing her the friendship of Cordelia Chase, the leader of Sunnydale High's in crowd. Rupert Giles, the new school librarian introduces himself as her new Watcher. He knows that Buffy is the Slayer—the one girl in all the world with the strength and skill to hunt and kill vampires.

When a student is found dead in a locker—with bite marks on his neck and completely drained of his blood—Buffy investigates, and tells Giles about the body, but says that she no longer wants to be a Slayer. According to Giles a crucial mystical convergence is about to happen in Sunnydale, and that is why she has come there. When they leave, a bewildered Xander emerges from the library stacks—Buffy's secret is out.

Later, in a subterranean chamber we see a vampire (Luke), kneeling in front of a pool of blood saying *"The sleeper will awaken. And the world will bleed."*

As Buffy prepares for her night out at the Bronze, Sunnydale's hippest (and apparently only) nightclub, Joyce is full of optimism about their new life in Sunnydale. On her way to the Bronze, Buffy is followed by a handsome, mysterious stranger (Angel). She ducks into an alley and after some martial arts mayhem Angel convinces her that he doesn't bite. Sunnydale is located on the Hellmouth—a focal point for demonic activity—and he says she must be ready for 'The Harvest.' He throws her a packet, which she opens to find a crucifix.

At the Bronze, Giles convinces her to use her power to try to sense if there are any vampires in the Bronze. Buffy *does* spot a vampire, talking to Willow, who then leaves with him. Buffy grabs a makeshift stake, runs after them, turns a corner and attacks... Cordelia, pretty much destroying any chance for popularity at Sunnydale High School.

Jesse, Xander's buddy, is chatting with the vampire we saw at the episode start, now looking like a normal student, Darla. Back at the pool of blood, something distinctly unpleasant breaks through the surface and rises: the demonic Master. He is hungry and weak, and would like breakfast—just something light—and young!

Outside the Bronze Buffy enlists Xander in her hunt for Willow. The vampire has taken Willow to a mausoleum in the cemetery. As Willow tries to escape, Darla arrives with Jesse, who she has bitten. Buffy and Xander enter, Buffy promptly killing Willow's vampiric date and fighting Darla while Xander leads Willow and a weakened Jesse out to safety. Luke, the monstrous vampire we have seen attending to the Master, joins the battle. While they are fighting, Darla escapes to get Jesse, Xander and Willow.

Luke throws Buffy into a coffin, jumps in and leans in to bite her...

## The Harvest (03/10/97), Episode:4V02

Written by Joss Whedon, Directed by John Kretchmer.

...just as Luke is about to bite Buffy, he burns his hand on the cross given to her by Angel and she escapes, saving Xander and Willow. Darla and Luke take Jesse to the Master.

Giles and Buffy tell Xander and Willow about the life of a Slayer and the truth about vampires and demons. Willow uses the Internet to find the underground tunnels the vampires use. Buffy goes after Jesse, offending Xander by telling him that it's her job, not his. Giles asks Willow to try and find more information about The Harvest.

As Buffy is about to enter the tunnels. Angel appears and warns her against going down there—The Harvest will be that night. Descending into the Master's domain Buffy is horrified to find Xander has followed her. They find Jesse, who leads them into a room with no way out; Buffy and Xander turn to find that Jesse's a vampire—and he likes it. Buffy ejects him from the room and escapes with Xander through a grating and heads back to the library. The Master is furious that the Slayer has escaped and with his own blood paints a three-pointed star on Luke's forehead.

Giles and Willow have discovered at The Harvest, the Master can draw power from one of his followers as the follower feeds, and can break through to our reality.

At the Bronze Luke and the vampire horde enter and take control of the club. By the time Buffy reaches the Bronze, Luke and the vampires have begun The Harvest, and the Master is gaining strength from each killing. Buffy fights with Luke while Xander, Willow and Giles sneak people out through the back.

Buffy tricks Luke by breaking a window and telling him the light from a streetlight is daylight. He is distracted long enough for Buffy to stake him.

The Master is too weak to rise and The Harvest has been stopped. Angel says, *"She did it. I'll be damned."*

## The Witch (03/17/97), Episode:4V03

Written by Dana Reston Directed by Stephen Cragg.

In a last-ditch attempt at normality Buffy decides to try out for cheerleading. As one girl auditions, her hands catch fire and Buffy puts them out. Amy feels pressured to make the squad, as her mother, Catherine, was a cheerleading champion at Sunnydale High. Cordelia makes the squad, but Amy is upset at being third alternate—with Buffy as first alternate.

Amy's mom's has a trophy in the school display case—a model of a cheerleader. The next day at Driver's Ed training Cordelia goes blind and crashes her car into a fence and is rescued from possible death by Buffy. Giles is certain that witchcraft is behind these incidents. Amy is the obvious suspect, and Xander and Willow test her with a potion that turns a witch's skin blue, with positive results. Instantaneously another cheerleader in the suddenly has no mouth, but Amy is horrified, making Buffy doubt whether Amy realises what she's doing.

At cheerleading practice, Buffy acts strangely; she throws the captain across the gym and is kicked off the squad. It's time for the next alternate to come in—Amy. As Xander and Willow take Buffy out of the gym she faints. Her life is slowly fading away; Giles says she only has a few hours left and they need Amy's spell book to save her. At Amy's house they find Amy—in the body of her mother. Amy's mother, Catherine, is the witch, and has switched bodies with her daughter to relive her glory days as a cheerleader. They rush back to the science lab with Amy and the spell book.

As the counterspell begins 'Amy' charges out of the gym to stop it. The spell is completed as she arrives and the two switch back to their old bodies. Buffy revives and fights Catherine, who casts a spell to send Buffy to hell. Buffy deflects it with a mirror and Catherine disappears. Amy goes to live with her dad. As they pass the trophy case, we catch a glimpse of Catherine's cheerleading trophy. Its eyes are moving...

*Continuity:* After Catherine Madison is defeated, Giles says, *"It was my first casting,"* a statement proved wrong by the events of *The Dark Age.*

## Teacher's Pet (03/25/97), Episode:4V04

Written by David Greenwalt, Directed by Bruce Seth Green.

Angel sees Buffy at the Bronze and warns her about the vampire who left a triple wound on his arm, who she tastefully christens Fork Guy. In biology class, Dr Gregory tells Buffy he wants to prove wrong everyone who doubts her ability to succeed in school. The following day, Dr Gregory turns up *sans* head, and new (and gorgeous) substitute teacher, Ms Natalie French, puts the male members of the class into love overdrive. Asking for after-school volunteers to help her model the egg sacks of the Praying Mantis, school jock Blayne is picked as her assistant for that day, Xander for the next.

Buffy spots a vampire with three claws for a hand, but he escapes. Later Buffy sees him stalk Ms French, but back off when he sniffs her, and he runs when she looks at him. Arriving late for Biology class the next day Buffy sees Ms French turn her head around—all the way around. Buffy and Giles believe that Ms French is actually a giant praying mantis.

Xander goes to Ms French's house, where she offers him a drink, and (surprise!) he passes out, waking up in her cellar to find Blayne in an adjoining cage. Ms French is now completely converted to her giant-mantis form, preparing egg sacks. Blayne has already seen her take a guy, lay her eggs, mate with him and bite his head off. Giles confirms there is a creature called a She-Mantis and Buffy suggests that bat sonar might disrupt the She-Mantis's system. When they get to Ms French's house they find the wrong woman—she's used a retired teacher's records. Buffy retrieves Fork Guy from the sewers to sniff out the She-Mantis; he winces when they reach the right house. Buffy kills him with a handy fence slat when he turns on her.

Buffy crashes through the window into the basement, using insecticide to fend off the She-Mantis. Giles plays the bat sonar and Buffy chops her to pieces with a machete. Afterwards, Willow mentions the fact that the mantis only chose virgins. Blayne offers to sue anyone who repeats that. Xander vents his spleen using the machete to hack the egg sacks to pieces.

The next day in biology, there is a new, strict teacher. Buffy finds Dr Gregory's glasses and puts them away in the closet. There is a sack of hatching eggs under one of the shelves...

## Never Kill A Boy On The First Date (03/31/97), Episode:4V05

Written by Rob Des Hotel & Dean Batali, Directed by David Semel.

Buffy and Giles find a ring left behind by a vampire she's slain, while the Master explains that the Anointed One will rise from the ashes of five dead to lead the Slayer into Hell. Giles discovers the ring is from the Order of Aurelius, and recounts the same prophecy. Owen, a shy, bookish student is smitten with Buffy and asks her to the Bronze that night. Buffy and Giles stake out graveyard to see if the Anointed One will rise that night and by the time Buffy gets to the Bronze, Cordelia has taken advantage of her absence and is dancing very closely with Owen. An airport shuttle bus crashes and five people survive the wreck, only to be killed by vampires.

The next day, Owen asks Buffy out again. As she leaves Giles shows up with a newspaper about the killing; five died as the prophecy described, and one of them was wanted for murder. He insists that they check it out, but she refuses and goes on her date with Owen.

Giles goes to the funeral home and ends up barricaded in, pursued by vampires. Willow and Xander find him and go and get Buffy to come to the funeral home. Owen follows them there and Buffy asks Xander and Willow to look after him, leaving them in the Observatory, hoping they'll be safe. After they barricade the door shut, the killer from the bus rises from a gurney as a vampire.

Buffy finds Giles hiding on top of a corpse in a storage room and tries to explain the situation to him. As the three friends escape from the Observatory they find Buffy. She returns to the storage room where Giles inadvertently starts the incinerator. Buffy fights the vampire; Owen enters and clumsily tackles him, giving Buffy a reprieve. The vampire attacks Owen, leaving him for dead. Buffy, furious her date has been killed finishes the vampire off by incinerating him.

Owen is not dead, just unconscious; unfortunately the experience has turned him into a danger freak. Realising she could get him killed, Buffy gives him a 'let's just be friends' speech. Buffy and Giles believe that they have killed the Anointed—but they are wrong. The Anointed One did rise. We see the Master welcoming Collin, an eight-year old boy from the bus accident…

## The Pack (04/07/97), Episode:4V06

Written by Matt Kiene & Joe Reinkmeyer, Directed by Bruce Seth Green.

On a school trip to the Sunnydale Zoo, four 'cool' students—the pack—grab the bookish Lance's notebook, forcing him to follow them into the new hyena exhibit. Xander goes to his rescue. Buffy and Willow follow but are stopped by a zookeeper; the hyenas just came in from Africa and are in quarantine. As the four bullies push Lance towards the hyenas. Xander arrives and they are caught by the glare from the hyenas' eyes. The eyes of Xander and the bullies glow brightly and they all start to laugh—they've stepped into a mystical circle on the floor and a transformation has begun.

Back at school, Principal Flutie introduces the students to a little pig—Herbert, the Sunnydale Razorbacks' new mascot. Herbert reacts strangely to Xander, who has become more confident and aggressive since the zoo trip. He sniffs at Buffy, and at the Bronze he eats her food. He's become nasty, moody and aggressive. Giles thinks Xander a normal teenager, saying *"It's devastating—he's turned into a sixteen-year-old boy. Of course, you'll have to kill him."*

The pack and Xander break into the classroom and start to tease Herbert the pig… Later Herbert is found dead—eaten. Giles concedes that there is something wrong with Xander and the other four. Research seems to indicate that the spirits of the hyenas were transported into the five. Buffy finds Xander, who pounces on her and makes vigorous sexual advances. Buffy decks him with a desk, drags him unconscious back to the library and locks him up. Principal Flutie orders the rest of the pack to his office, where, after a frank and fair exchange of views, they eat him.

Giles tells them about 'Primals'—animal worshippers who can draw the spirits of animals into themselves. The spirits of the hyenas must be returned to the animals. Giles and Buffy decide they need more information from the zookeeper and ask Willow to stay with Xander. Xander tries to get the keys from her, but she's clever enough to keep them.

A suspiciously knowledgeable zookeeper says all the students must return to the mystical circle in the hyena cage. Buffy and Giles discover that the pack will come looking for its lost member before feeding. Buffy rushes back in time to save Willow; the pack has already broken Xander out of the cage.

Buffy save a family from attack by the pack, while at the zoo the zookeeper, who was trying to transport the hyena sprits into himself, knocks Giles out. He grabs Willow in order to perform the 'predatory act' which is part of the ritual. Xander, back to his old self, dives at the zookeeper, and frees Willow. When the zookeeper fights Buffy, she hurls him into the hyena cage; they eat him. The next day, Xander apologises for anything he may have done while a hyena and pretends to not remember anything about his attack on Buffy. After the girls leave, Giles says he doesn't know of any memory loss associated with the Primal state. Xander asks him to keep that their little secret.

*The Verdict:* One of the episodes that give a clue about how *Buffy* will progress: the sheer cheek of building up Principal Flutie, to have him eaten by a group of high-schoolers is evil and very, very funny.

## Angel (04/14/97), Episode:4V07

Written by: David Greenwalt, Directed by: Scott Brazil.

Buffy decides to leave the Bronze but feels as if someone is following her. Outside she is attacked by three vampires, who drag her into an alleyway as she tries to fight them off. As one leans in to feed, Angel appears and fights alongside her. Angel is injured in the ribs by an iron bar. The Master has sent 'The Three' against her.

Angel and Buffy escape safely to her house, where she tends to his wound. Angel meets Buffy's mom and between them they manage to convince her to go to bed. Buffy says a loud goodbye and closes the door, but Angel stays inside and spends the night in her bedroom, sleeping next to her bed The Three can't come in unless they're invited. Giles identifies Buffy's attackers as warrior vampires. She must be causing the Master much trouble for him to send The Three—they must start training with weapons.

Darla kills The Three for failing the Master. Buffy finds a crossbow, but Giles insists they start with the quarterstaff and work up to the crossbow. After a fight ending with him on his behind he changes his mind. At night, Buffy brings Angel food that she's concealed at the dinner table. Angel says that he can't be around her—when he is, all he wants to do is kiss her. They kiss but Angel can't control the demon inside of him and reveals his other self. Angel is a vampire. Buffy screams and Angel flies out of the window and slides down the roof.

Buffy tells Giles and friends about Angel being a vampire, hoping that Giles knows of a way that a vampire could be good. Giles offers no hope for her. As Angel arrives back at his apartment and turns on the light Darla comes out of the shadows and reminds him of his past with her. While Angel attempts to convince her that he's not evil any more, she notices his refrigerated supply of pig's blood.

Darla goes to Buffy's and attacks Joyce. Angel bursts in to stop her, and she throws Joyce at him. Buffy comes home to find Joyce in Angel's arms. She assumes the obvious and attacks him, causing him to flee. Buffy takes Joyce to the hospital and then goes to kill Angel, despite her love for him. Armed with a crossbow she finds Angel at the Bronze. He explains that he has committed many dreadful acts over the course of his lifetime, but his soul has been restored by a curse laid on him after feeding on a gypsy girl. Now he is haunted by his past horrors. For the past hundred years, he hasn't fed off a living human being.

Buffy offers her neck, but he refuses. Darla comes out of the shadows armed with two guns, and fires at Angel; he falls. Buffy and Darla fight until Angel shoots her with the crossbow. Buffy and Angel agree their love can't work, and enjoy a good-bye kiss. Buffy walks away and we see that the cross Buffy wears has burned its shape into Angel's neck.

*The Verdict:* This is a key episode, that introduces not just the fact of Angel's vampirism, but his history with other vampires and the curse, that will form a strong part of the story arcs of the next two seasons.

## I, Robot—You Jane (04/28/97), Episode:4V08

Written by Ashley Gable & Thomas A Swyden, Directed by Stephen Posey.

Cartona Italy, 1418. A young man approaches a demon called Moloch the Corrupter, who smiles at him and then snaps his neck. A group of monks trap Moloch in a book, words appearing on the pages as the book takes him.

Buffy opens a crate in the library and pulls out the book. Willow and Xander and two students Fritz and Dave, are helping Jenny Calendar, the computer science teacher, to scan books into the school computer system. Willow scans the book containing Moloch and as she does the characters disappear from its pages. As she turns away from the computer the words 'Where am I?' appear onscreen.

Willow is having an online romance with a boy called Malcolm. When Buffy asks Dave about Malcolm, Dave tells Buffy to leave Willow alone. Buffy follows Dave to a closed computer research building; the place is crawling with people working. Willow is having an online chat with Malcolm when he mentions Buffy's expulsion. Willow doesn't understand how he knows about this, and quickly ends their conversation. When Buffy looks for Willow in the computer lab, Dave directs her to the girls' locker room where Fritz has set up a trap to electrocute. As Buffy arrives he turns on the water and leaves. Dave warns Buffy but she still receives a jolt of electricity before she can escape. Dave refuses to work for Moloch anymore, but the printer is printing a suicide note—his own. Fritz appears behind him.

In the library, Giles explains to Buffy and Xander about trapping demons in books, and that scanning the book released Moloch into the computer, where he now has access to any computer in the world. Buffy tries to delete the files Moloch, who appears on the screen and warns Buffy to stay away from Willow. Buffy finally makes the connection that Moloch is Malcolm. Dave's body is found hanging from the ceiling of the lab.

While Buffy and Xander rush to save Willow, a desperate Giles asks Ms Calendar for help and discovers she is a techno-pagan with extensive knowledge of the mystical realm and the events around Sunnydale. Learning about the Slayer and the demon Moloch, Ms Calendar uses the internet to form an energy circle so they can perform the ritual to stop him.

Willow has been taken to the research facility, where Moloch is in a robotic incarnation of his demonic self. He breaks Fritz's neck and is about to kill Willow when the spell begins to take effect. Instead of sending him back to the book, the spell traps him in his robot body. Moloch attacks Buffy, who tricks him into hitting a high voltage junction box. He short-circuits and blows up. Exit one demon.

*The Verdict:* An entertaining but uninspired episode, notable only for introducing Jenny Calendar as an occasional team member.

## The Puppet Show (05/05/97), Episode:4V09

Written by Dean Batali & Rob Des Hotel, Directed by Ellen Pressman.

Buffy, Xander and Willow are caught mocking the talent show that Giles is organising by the new principal, who punishes them by insisting they participate. *"Mr Flutie may have gone in for all that touchy-feely relating nonsense, but he was eaten."*

As the withdrawn Morgan performs his ventriloquist act, his dummy Sid starts to delivers amusing lines, almost as if someone else were operating him…

One of the dancers is found dead, with her heart removed. Buffy questions Morgan, and overhears the dummy apparently warning him. When Buffy goes to sleep that night, Sid is outside her window. She wakes as she senses him enter her room. Coming back up from inspecting under her bed, she sees Sid there, screams, and knocks him off of the bed. Sid runs away.

Giles has found that there is a brotherhood of seven demons who take the form of young humans, but need human organs, a brain and a heart, every seven years, or revert to their original form.

Buffy encounters Principal Snyder snooping around backstage and finds Morgan dead, with his brain removed. She is toppled by a falling chandelier and when she regains consciousness Sid is there with a kitchen knife. Buffy overpowers him, but realises that they have each mistaken the other for a demon. Sid was a human who hunted demons, having his spirit placed into the dummy for his troubles. The demon who cursed him is in the talent show—if Sid can kill him, he'll be free. Morgan's brain falls from the catwalk—Morgan had brain cancer—so the demon still needs a healthy brain. A student, Marc, convinces Giles to fill in for his assistant in his guillotine act (!). As he lies tied in the guillotine Giles realises he's about to get his brains removed, but it's too late—Marc begins to slash at the rope that holds the blade up. Buffy drop kicks Marc away from the rope and Marc begins to change into a demon.

The rope snaps but Xander grabs it and stops the blade. Marc becomes more and more powerful as he reverts to his demonic self. Giles gets clear of the guillotine as Sid jumps onto the demon's back and begins stabbing with his knife. Buffy does a full sidekick to the demon, he staggers back and lands with his neck in the guillotine. Xander lets the rope go, and the blade chops off the demon's head. Sid plunges the knife into the demon's heart and slumps over the body, just a lifeless puppet.

Buffy gently lifts Sid and holds him in her arms. She starts to walk off stage, when the curtain is drawn, the now full auditorium catching them all in a tableau. They all stare out nervously. Principal Snyder has the last word:

*"I don't get it. What is it? Avant-garde?"*

*Quote of the show: "This place has quite a reputation. Suicide, missing persons, spontaneous cheerleader combustion… You can't put up with that. You've gotta keep an eye on the bad element."* —Principal Snyder.

## Nightmares (05/12/97), Episode:4V10

Story by Joss Whedon, Teleplay by David Greenwalt, Directed by Bruce Seth Green.

Buffy has a vivid nightmare about being attacked by the Master, but is awakened by Joyce just as he is about to bite her. Buffy's dad is coming to visit her. In class, Wendell opens his book and spiders emerge and attack him, observed by a young boy standing outside the classroom window. The Master explains to the Anointed One that fear is the most powerful force in the world, and a powerful, psychic force is happening above.

Wendell loves spiders, but has had recurring nightmares about attacks since he left his collection with his brother, who left their heat lamp on for a week and killed them, and that's when his nightmares started. As Buffy takes a test she glances at the clock and sees the entire hour is almost up. Around her the students rise and begin turning their tests in. The child appears at the door and looks in at Buffy with a sad look on his face.

A student is attacked by a huge scarred man who says the

words 'Lucky Nineteen,' during the attack. At the hospital Buffy and Giles discover that she is the second victim of the attacker, the first is still in a coma. Other incidents happen at school: a tough punk's reputation is destroyed by the appearance of his mollycoddling mother, Xander finds he's only wearing boxer shorts, Giles has forgotten how to read. Showing Buffy the paper he can't read she sees the picture of the little boy who keeps appearing around these incidents.

Twelve-year-old Billy Palmer is the coma victim found beaten and unconscious after his little league game on Saturday. His uniform number is 19. Giles posits that Buffy has been seeing his astral body. Buffy's father enters the library looking for her, and outside explains he left home because Buffy caused so much trouble and was such a disappointment to him. He leaves Buffy in shock—and the boy appears again.

They realise that the boy in the hospital is making their nightmares come true using the power of the Hellmouth. Soon everyone in Sunnydale will face their own worst nightmare. Outside the school Buffy sees Billy, who tells her that the Ugly Man wants to kill him. Lucky Nineteen is what the Ugly Man calls him. The Ugly Man appears and attacks Buffy.

Giles warns Xander and Willow that Buffy doesn't realise what's happening and that given the nature of what she's likely to have nightmares about, they must find her.

Buffy escapes from the Ugly Man with Billy and temporarily traps him. Billy says this is how it always happens. Billy is unnerved by some nearby baseball players—Buffy learns that when you lose at baseball it's bad.

Willow and Xander's attempts to find Buffy lead them into their own nightmares, as Buffy and Billy manage to escape Ugly Man by pushing through some bushes and jumping from school during the day into a cemetery at night.

The Master appears and shoves Buffy into an open grave, burying her as he does so.

Xander and Willow escape from their nightmares and meet Giles who says that in a few hours reality will become the realm of nightmares. A cemetery has appeared across from the school, shrouded in permanent night. In the cemetery Giles sees a gravestone that reads: *Buffy Summers 1981—1997*. As Giles realises that it's his nightmare, Buffy emerges—as a vampire.

If they can wake up Billy, Giles believes the nightmares will stop and reality will shift back into place. They return to the hospital and Ugly Man appears again. Buffy beats the tar out of him and asks Billy to finish the job. Billy looks down at the Ugly Man and reaches for his neck. He peels back the Ugly Man's face and a bright light streams out. In the next instant everything changes—the Ugly Man is gone, Buffy, Xander and Willow are themselves again and Billy wakes up.

His little league coach enters and is shocked to find the boy awake. Buffy confronts him about beating up the boy for losing a game and when he tries to flee, Xander grabs him. Buffy's dad shows up after school and cheerfully greets her and as she leaves with him, Xander is forced to confess to Willow that he still dug Buffy, even as a vampire.

## Invisible Girl (05/19/97), Episode:4V11

Story by Joss Whedon, Teleplay by Ashley Gable & Thomas A. Swyden, Directed by Reza Badiyi.

As the Spring Fling dance draws near, Cordelia's boyfriend Mitch is beaten up in the school locker-room—by a baseball bat wielded by an invisible assailant. The attacker leaves the cryptic message 'Look' scrawled on the lockers. As Buffy says, monsters don't usually send messages. It's pretty much 'crush, kill, destroy'. This is different.

Giles suggests it might be an invisible creature, ghost or poltergeist. Willow agrees to prepare a list of dead or missing kids, to see if they can work out who the ghost is.

When another attack finds Cordelia's friend Harmony flying backwards down a flight of stairs, Buffy hears laughter and footsteps and pursues the invisible attacker into the band room. She is bumped into by the invisible girl, and calls out to her, to no response. She doesn't notice a ceiling hatch raise and lower.

Buffy asks Giles if he's ever touched a ghost and Giles say from what he's read it's a cold feeling. Buffy says the 'ghost' bumped into her—she thinks they are looking for an invisible girl.

Angel talks to Giles about Buffy—he knows that something big is about to happen. Giles is antipathetic to the vampire, but excited to find that Angel can obtain the lost Pergamum Codex, containing prophecies about the Slayer's role in the end years. (This will lead straight into the events of the next episode, *Prophecy Girl*.)

Cordelia is elected May Queen for the school dance and Buffy is convinced Cordelia is the link between the two mysterious attacks. Using Willow's information Buffy thinks Marcie Ross may be the girl. Marcie was a flautist with the school band. In the band room Buffy notices a footprint on a chair and makes her way into the ceiling partition to where the invisible girl has been hiding, and finds Marcie's yearbook.

Cordelia's teacher is almost suffocated as a plastic bag is slipped over her head and tied off, only rescued by the appearance of a tardy Cordelia. On the board behind her is chalked the word 'Listen'. No one seems to remember that Marcie existed. Giles tells them that physics theorises that reality is shaped by our perception, and with the Hellmouth below sending out mystical energy, people perceived Marcie as invisible, and she became so.

Marcie's goal seems to be the destruction of Cordelia and Cordelia's coronation as May Queen that evening will be the perfect place for Marcie to attack. As Buffy forces Cordelia to get ready for the dance in a mop closet, Marcie yanks her up into the ceiling, followed by Buffy. Giles, Willow and Xander have been lured to the boiler room where they discover—a tape recorder.

Xander: *"Can you say 'gulp'?"*

Marcie slams the door behind her and runs off, leaving the trio trapped with only the sound of escaping gas for company.

Buffy and Cordelia are injected with an anaesthetic by Marcie and wake in the Bronze to find themselves tied to the King and Queen of the May thrones. On the curtain in front of them is the word 'Learn'. Marcie, armed with a tray of surgical instruments, explains to that she intends to give Cordelia a face no one will ever forget. Buffy manages to free herself and a scuffle ensues, with Buffy finally knocking Marcie out, just as a pair of FBI agents arrive to take away. The FBI men promise to 'rehabilitate' Marcie.

Giles Xander and Willow are saved by a late-breaking Angel but Giles tells Buffy it was a janitor—he doesn't want to remind Buffy of her lost love. Our last sight of Marcie is her being introduced to her (invisible) classmates by the two FBI agents. Marcie opens her book and flips through to page fifty-four. The

title of chapter eleven reads 'Assassination and Infiltration'.
Marcie: *"Cool!"*

### Prophecy Girl (06/02/97), Episode:4V12

Written & Directed by Joss Whedon.

Giles is reading the Pergamum Codex, promised to him by Angel in *Invisible Girl,* and is visibly unnerved by what he reads there about the Master and the Slayer. Moments an earthquake rocks the building. The Master exults, claiming they are in the final days.

Buffy tells Giles that the vampires are increasing in boldness—they are nearly at the school. Giles pays little attention, obviously distracted by his own thoughts. Xander finally gets the nerve to ask her out, but she turns him down, saying she doesn't think of him 'that way'. Xander says he guesses a guy's gotta be undead to make time with Buffy.

Giles and Ms Calendar discuss the prophecy, Jenny stating that it's indicative of an approaching apocalypse. Buffy finds blood running from the washroom taps. Going to tell Giles she overhears Giles telling Angel, *"Tomorrow night Buffy will face the Master, and she will die."* Buffy confronts Giles and Angel asking *"They say how he's gonna kill me? Do you think it'll hurt?"*. As tears roll down her face she yanks the cross from her neck and tells them she doesn't want to die—she's sixteen years old and she doesn't want to die.

At home, Joyce gives Buffy a beautiful white sleeveless gown that that she'd seen her admiring for the dance.

Cordelia and Willow discover Kevin and a roomful of fellow students killed by vampires.

Willow: *"I'm not okay. I knew those guys. I go to that room every day. And when I walked in there, it... it wasn't our world anymore. They made it theirs. And they had fun. What are we gonna do?"*

Buffy: *"What we have to. Promise me you'll stay in tonight, okay?"*

At last Giles figures out that the vampire Buffy killed in *Never Kill a Boy on the First Date* wasn't the Anointed. Buffy arrives and tells Giles that she is going. He intends to go in her place but she knocks him out, retrieves her cross, and leaves, crossbow in hand.

Outside the school she takes the hand of the Anointed One as he leads her to the Master. Xander uses a cross to force Angel to lead him to the Master.

Xander: *"I don't like you. At the end of the day, I pretty much think you're a vampire. But Buffy's got this big old yen for you. She thinks you're a real person. And right now I need you to prove her right."*

Giles, Jenny and Willow work out that the Hellmouth will appear at the Bronze if Buffy isn't successful. At the entrance to the Master's lair Collin points down, inviting her to enter. The Master's voice welcomes her, and he steps into the light. Buffy launches a bolt in the direction of his voice, but he catches it in mid-flight. The Master is behind her; she turns and the crossbow is knocked out of her hands. The Master holds his hand out to her and she is inexorably pulled back by his hypnotic powers. He removes her leather jacket, leaving her dressed in the white prom gown. He tells her that prophecies are tricky creatures—she is the one that will set him free! If she hadn't come, he couldn't leave. He bites her, taking a few sips and drops her face down into a pool of water. His confines dissolve in light and energy. He leaves for the surface.

Angel and Xander arrive and Xander begins trying to resuscitate the drowned Buffy. Jenny and Willow have been waylaid by vampires, only to be rescued by Cordelia, who takes them back to the school. Giles is baffled as to why all the vampires appear to be heading his way. His questions are resolved when a many tentacled monster forces its way through the library floor—his calculations were wrong, the Hellmouth will appear at his library.

Xander's successfully revives Buffy; she feels stronger, different and heads off for a second confrontation with the Master. At the school she fights the disconcerted Master on the roof, and she throws him through the library roof window to be impaled on a table. He disintegrates, and the monster and vampires leave with him. The Master is defeated, and the Hellmouth is closed—for now.

Buffy: *"We saved the world. I say we party. I mean, I got all pretty!"*

## Season Two

### Regular Cast

Sarah Michelle Gellar (Buffy Summers), Nicholas Brendon (Xander Harris), Alyson Hannigan (Willow Rosenberg), Charisma Carpenter (Cordelia Chase), David Boreanaz (Angel), Anthony Stewart Head (Rupert Giles), James Marsters (Spike), Juliet Landau (Drusilla).

### Production Staff Credits

Executive Producer: Joss Whedon , Co-Producer: David Solomon, Consulting Producer: Howard Gordon (5V01-5V13), Producer: Gareth Davies, Executive Producers: Sandy Gallin; Gail Berman; Fran Rubel Kuzui; Kaz Kuzui, Co-Executive Producer: David Greenwalt , Executive Story Editors: Rob Des Hotel & Dean Batali, Story Editor: Marti Noxon (5V14-5V22), Unit Production Manager/Co-Producer: Gary Law, First Assistant Director: Brenda Kalosh (all odd-numbered episodes and 5V22); Ken Collins (5V02); Robert D. Nellans (all even-numbered episodes, 5V04-5V20), Second Assistant Director: Randy LaFollette (5V01-5V08); Alan Steinman (5V09-5V22), Score: Christophe Beck (5V01, 5V04, 5V06, 5V08, 5V11, 5V13, 5V14, 5V16, 5V17, 5V19, 5V21, 5V22, additional music 5V02); Adam Fields (5V02); Shawn K. Clement & Sean Murray (5V03, 5V05, 5V07, 5V09, 5V10, 5V12, 5V15, 5V18, 5V20), Theme: Nerf Herder, Director of Photography: Michael Gershman (all but 5V16, 5V17); Kenneth D. Zunder, A.S.C. (5V16, 5V17), Production Designer: Carey Meyer, Editor: Regis B. Kimble (5V01, 5V04, 5V07, 5V10, 5V13, 5V16, 5V19); Kimberly Ray (5V02, 5V05, 5V08, 5V11, 5V14, 5V17, 5V20, 5V22); Skip MacDonald (5V03, 5V06, 5V09, 5V12, 5V15, 5V18, 5V21), Casting: Marcia Shulman, C.S.A., Costume Designer: Cynthia Bergstrom, Production Sound Mixer: Maury Harris, C.A.S. (5V01-5V14); Robert Eber, C.A.S. (5V15-5V22), Art Director: Stephanie J. Gordon (5V01-5V10), Set Designer: Caroline Quinn (5V11-5V22), Set Decorator: David Koneff, Leadman: Gustav Gustafson, Construction Coordinator: Steve West, Paint Foreman: Lisa Gamel, Property Master Ken Wilson, Chief Lighting Technician: Dayton Nietert, Key Grip: Tom Keefer, Camera Operator: Russ McElhatton (5V01-5V04); Eyal Gordin (5V05-5V13); Herbert Davis (5V14-5V22), Script Supervisor: Lesley King (5V01-5V05, all odd-numbered episodes, 5V07-5V21, 5V22); Kelly Akers (all even-numbered episodes, 5V06-5V20), Location Manager: Jordana Kronen, Production Auditor: Edwin L. Perez, Stunt Coordinator: Dean Ferrandini (5V01); Jeff Pruitt (5V02-5V22), Transportation Coordinator: Robert Ellis, Costume Supervisor: Karen Hudson (5V01-5V03); Donna Barrish (5V04, 5V05), Hair Stylist: Jeri Baker, Make-Up Artist: John Maldonado, Special Effects Coordinator: Bruce Minkus (5V13-5V22), Production Coordinator: Phyllis Saldutti, Script Coordinator: Amy Wolfram (5V01-5V15); David Goodman (5V16-5V22), Assistant to Joss Whedon: George Snyder (5V01-5V17); Diego Gutierrez (5V18-5V22), Assistant to Gail Berman: Caroline Kallas, Assistant to David Greenwalt: Robert Price, Assistant to Gareth Davies: Marc D. Alpert, Post

Production Coordinator: Brian Wankum, Assistant Editor: Marilyn Adams (all odd-numbered episodes); Golda Savage (all even-numbered episodes), Post Production Sound: TODD AO STUDIO, Supervising Sound Editor: Cindy Rabideau, Re-Recording Mixers: Kevin Patrick Burns; Todd Keith Orr; Peter Nusbaum (5V01-5V08); Jim Fitzpatrick (5V09, 5V10, 5V15-5V20); Don DiGirolamo (5V11-5V14); Chris Minkler (5V21, 5V22), Music Editor: Fernand Bos, Special Make-Up Effects: John Vulich, Make-Up Supervisor: Todd McIntosh, Visual Effects: POP (5V04 only), Visual Effects Supervisors: Michael Peterson & Alex Eglis (5V04 only), Vampire Design Evolved From Concepts Created by: The Burman Studios, Post Production Services and Visual Effects: Digital Magic, Main Title Design: Montgomery/Cobb, Processing: Four Media Company.

## Season 2 Episodes

### When She Was Bad (09/15/97), Episode:5V01

Written & Directed by Joss Whedon.

While Xander and Willow discuss the missing Buffy they are attacked by a vampire; a hand pulls the vampire off Xander. It's Buffy, who drops the vampire, and turns to Willow and Xander:

Buffy: *"Hi, guys!"*

Buffy turns her attention back to the vampire, who gets up in time to be impaled on a dead branch, bursting into ashes.

Buffy: *"Miss me?"*

It's a darker Buffy who has returned to Sunnydale. The near-massacre of prom night and her own death at the hands of the Master have left the Slayer unnerved, and she suffers terrible nightmares of his return.

The Master is not necessarily as dead as everyone thinks, as the Anointed One plots to bring him back. He needs to assemble those who were there when he died—Willow, Cordelia, Giles, and Jenny Calendar. Angel tries to warn Buffy about the Anointed One's powers, but she is deliberately cool to him. She is efficiently nasty to Cordelia (*"You won't tell anyone that I'm the Slayer, and I won't tell anyone you're a moron."*), she is cold to Willow and Xander, and tries to make Angel jealous by dancing seductively with Xander. Leaving Buffy, Cordelia is kidnapped by vampires.

Giles is conjecturing that Buffy still hasn't dealt with the after effects of the events of *Prophecy Girl*, just as Buffy arrives. Buffy, still in major strop mode, receives a note, along with Cordelia's bracelet, instructing her to go to the Bronze if she wants to save ordelia. She refuses to take the others with her, saying she an't look after the three of them while she's fighting. At the ronze, Angel and Buffy find a vampire—not Cordelia. It is a rap for the four people present when the Master died; Cordelia, enny, Giles and Willow. Buffy rushes back to find a beaten ander, who threatens to kill her if Willow is harmed.

Buffy tortures the vampire at the Bronze to discover where he Anointed One is. Arriving there she finds Willow, Cordelia, iles and Jenny hung upside down over the Master's bones. he fights the Anointed One's vampires while Angel and Xander ree the others. Buffy gives the vampires such a beating that iles suggests she is 'working off her issues', finally killing the nointed One's lieutenant Absalom and using his ledgehammer to reduce the Master's bones to a fine powder. he bursts into tears as she drops the sledgehammer on the loor.

When she enters class the next day she's relieved to find that Villow and Xander have saved her a seat and (happily) things are ack to normal.

*The Verdict:* This show, like season three's *Dead Man's Party*, and ny episode with the whiny Joyce, is another examination of the ay that Buffy's role as a Slayer may lead her to be less than onsiderate of other peoples feelings. What a revelation—a sixteen-ear-old who's saved the world a few times can be a bit stroppy nd selfish. Here's a newflash: no world-saving necessary for the roduction of inconsiderate teenagers.

None of these kind of episodes are really successful, as they're logical; she puts her friends at risk every week. As in *Dead Man's arty* her 'concerned friends' come across as people in severe need f a reality check rather than the bunch of teenage social workers hat Wheedon seems to want. Especially funny is Cordelia lecturing uffy about her attitude(!)

*Quote of the show:* Cordelia: *"It stays with you forever. No matter hat they tell you, none of that rust and blood and grime comes out. I ean, you can dry clean till judgement day, you are living with those tains."*

Jenny: *"Yeah that's the worst part of being hung upside down by a ampire who wants to slit your throat: the stains."*

## Some Assembly Required (09/22/97), Episode:5V02

Written by Ty King, Directed by Bruce Seth Green.

The opening scene is classic Buffy: grue with tongue planted firmly in cheek. Angel tracks Buffy to the cemetery where they have a classic relationship argument while Buffy fights a newborn vampire. As she dispatches him Angel walks away:

Angel: *"Look, obviously I made a mistake coming here tonight."*

Buffy: *"Oh, no you don't. You can't just turn and walk away from me like that. It takes more than that to get rid of me."*

Following him she falls into an open grave. Angel assumes that another vampire has risen, but Buffy points out that no one has risen from the grave. Someone has been dragged from it.

Willow and Cordelia are preparing for the science fair. Willow asks advice from Chris, a science whiz who has become withdrawn since the death of his brother Daryl, while his creepy friend Eric takes photos of Cordelia. As Willow and Cordelia leave, Eric remarks that Cordelia would be perfect for them. Chris tells him not to be an idiot: she's alive.

The missing body is that of a dead cheerleader, Meredith, who died in a car accident with two other cheerleaders. They go to dig up the other two graves, to find the corpses missing. Meanwhile Cordelia stumbles upon a bunch of body parts in a dumpster, the parts adding up to three people—guess which three—but with some parts missing.

Due to the precision with which the bodies have been cut up, and the presence of books on anatomy and information about the three girls in his locker, the trail leads to Chris. We discover Chris and his buddy Eric have been secretly assembling a woman from these body parts for a resurrected (but rather ugly) Daryl, so he won't have to be alone. They don't yet have a head, and current favourites for donor are: Buffy, Willow and Cordelia.

Giles' attempts to court Ms Calendar are rescued when she in effect invites him to the school football game. Buffy finds the plans for the body in Chris's basement, with Cordelia's face pasted on top. She is observed by Daryl. Eric attempts to kill Cordelia as she changes for cheerleading. Buffy saves her and, as she talks to Chris, realises that Daryl is still alive. Daryl and Eric have kidnapped Cordelia and taken her to the old science lab, introducing her head to her body-to-be. Buffy arrives and mayhem ensues, ending with the spilling of a can of gasoline. A fire starts and Xander pushes Cordelia to safety. Daryl throws himself on the headless body and pledges his undying love as the flames consume them.

*The Verdict:* Welcome to another *Famous Monsters of Filmland*, Buffy-style, in this case a reprise of *Bride of Frankenstein*. Not a great episode plot wise, but some nice character interaction and the usual high standard of dialogue. There is a foreshadowing of Cordelia and Xander's forthcoming relationship in her realisation that he has risked his life to save her from the fire.

*Quote of the Week:* Buffy: *"I don't get it. Why go to all the trouble to dig up three girls only to chop them up and throw them away? It doesn't make any sense. Especially from a time management standpoint."*

## School Hard (09/29/97), Episode:5V03

Story by Joss Whedon & David Greenwalt, Teleplay by David Greenwalt, Directed by John T. Kretchmer.

Autumn is here and the time is right for... organising Parent Teacher Night, the punishment handed out to Buffy and another girl, Sheila, by Principal Snyder. There's two new vampires in town—Spike a blond, cropped haired English vampire and his 'significant other' Drusilla, a vampire weakened by some undocumented trouble in Prague. Spike is two hundred years old and has already killed two Slayers. He offers to kill Buffy for the Anointed One during the Night of St Vigeous, bringing power to the followers of the Master.

Buffy is preoccupied with trying to study, organise the night and cover for the permanently absent Sheila. Giles and Jenny Calendar have worked out that the forthcoming Saturday is the Night of St. Vigeous, although their calculations seem a tad uncertain.

Spike goes to the Bronze with some henchvampires (sorry, I promise I won't do that again) and studies the Slayer's form. On Parent Teacher Night, with Buffy frantically trying to keep her mother apart from Principal Snyder, Spike and his vampires turn up:

Spike: *"What can I say? I couldn't wait."*

Snyder convinces the parents and teachers that they are just being attacked by a drug-crazed gang (some drugs!). Buffy hides her mother while trying to defeat the vampires, and Giles tries to help Buffy, whose biggest worry is about her mother's safety. When the ever-helpful Sheila finally arrives— oh dear, she's a vampire too. Angel tries to fake Spike out by offering Xander as a sacrifice, but Spike isn't buying and attacks Angel, who we learn is the vampire who created Spike. Buffy turns up and fights Spike in what looks like a losing battle until Joyce (unwhiny for once, but incredibly credulous) whacks Spike in the head with an axe. Spike decides discretion is the better part of valour and runs. Buffy's resourcefulness in a crisis has impressed Joyce, despite Principal Snyder's negative assessment.

When Spike returns without a dead Slayer, the Anointed One is angry. In one of the great scenes that make *Buffy* a must-see, Spike first pretends to be humbled and then bursts into laughter and says if he had to do it again, he'd do exactly the same. Except he'd also... at this stage he picks up the Anointed One, throws him into a cage and raises it up to the light. The Anointed One screams and disappears in a puff of smoke.

Spike and Drusilla go to see what's on TV.

*The Verdict:* What is really another *Buffy* movie remake (*Die Hard* this time) is immensely enlivened by Spike (James Marsters, American but with a credible Brit accent coached by Anthony Steward Head) the first vampire in this series to suggest that it might actually be fun being bad. Spike's one-liners, his pragmatism, his love for Drusilla and above all his ability to send himself up make him one of the most compelling characters in the series so far.

### Inca Mummy Girl (10/06/97), Episode:5V04

Written by Matt Kiene & Joe Reinkemeyer, Directed by Ellen Pressman.

Sunnydale High's cultural exchange program is going fine until Xander discovers that Buffy's student is a guy. On a school museum trip a 500-year-old mummy is exhibited. The Incan people sacrificed their princess to the mountain god Sebancaya, an offering buried alive for eternity in the tomb, protected only by a cursed seal placed there as a warning to any who would wake her. Step forward idiot Rodney, who breaks the seal while trying to steal it. The mummy arises, grabs and kisses him and whoops, Rodney's a mummy. Trying to find him, Buffy, Giles, Xander and Willow go to the museum, where a man swings at Xander with a knife. Xander ducks and the man swings the other way, looks into the coffin and is obviously surprised by what he sees there. Xander fights the man off and he runs away. They identify the mummified Rodney by his braces. Giles tries to decipher what's left of the seal, but his resources aren't up to it.

Unknown to Buffy her exchange student is also a victim, and the mummy transforms into Ampata, a beautiful Peruvian teenage girl who then pretends to be Buffy's exchange student. It's love at first sight for Xander, and Giles asks her to help him decipher the seal. She says the picture of a man with a knife represents a bodyguard, and legend has it that he guards the mummy against those who would disturb her.

At the bleachers with Ampata, Xander is attacked by the bodyguard, who wants Xander to give him the seal. As Ampata screams the bodyguard recognises her. Xander kicks him off and they run away.

Ampata, shaken, tells Giles to destroy the seal but Giles wants to return to the museum to find the missing parts. The man from the museum confronts Ampata in the ladies room, and she kisses and mummifies him. While Xander takes Ampata to the school dance, Giles cross-references the pictograms and realises the man *was* a guard, but it was his job to ensure that the mummy didn't awaken and escape.

Buffy discovers her real exchange student's mummified corpse in her trunk. Giles and Buffy realise that Ampata's the mummy. Like Buffy, she was chosen to defend her people, and was killed at sixteen. At the dance Ampata is starting to turn back into a mummy. She must kiss someone quickly or it will be too late. She kisses Xander, but can't bring herself to kill him, so runs to the museum to try to break the seal that Giles is about to restore. Buffy stops Ampata from kissing Giles, but gets thrown into the tomb. When Ampata grabs Willow and tries to kiss her, Xander offers his own life instead. He keeps Ampata at bay until she begins to mummify, and is finally left holding her two withered arms as Buffy escapes from the tomb and pulls the now-mummified Ampata off him.

The next day Xander is really down, swearing he must have the worst taste in women of anyone in the world, ever. Buffy tells him that Ampata wasn't evil and she cared about Xander. She was just a girl, and she had her life taken away from her. Buffy remembers how she felt when she heard the prophecy that she was going to die—she wasn't obsessed with doing the right thing. Xander tells her that she gave up her life. Buffy says she had Xander to bring her back.

*The Verdict: The Mummy* gets the Buffy revamp this time, and adds another to the list of Xander's bizarre girlfriends. An average plot lifted by above average performances.

## Reptile Boy (10/13/97), Episode:5V05

Written and Directed by David Greenwalt.

As Buffy watches Indian movies with Xander and Willow at the Delta Zeta Kappa fraternity house, a young woman leaps from a second floor window, chased by fraternity brothers in robes. Running through the cemetery she is intercepted by a waiting brother and screams.

Giles worries about Buffy's attitude and orders her to train and patrol that night. Cordelia is making up to pair of fraternity guys, one of whom, Tom, is quite charming. Tom invites Buffy to a fraternity party the next night. Buffy declines out of loyalty to Angel. Patrolling the cemetery that night, Buffy finds a broken bracelet. Angel arrives and says there's blood on it—he can smell it. Buffy tell him it'd be nice to see him on an occasion that didn't involve blood and Angel explains he's trying to protect her. The conversation rapidly declines from there, culminating in Buffy deciding to go to the party. At the fraternity house a new brother is being inducted; chained to the wall is the girl they captured in the graveyard.

Buffy gives Giles the bracelet, saying a combination of homework and a sick mom means she can't patrol. Her lying to Giles upsets Willow, and Xander resolves to crash the party. At the party, Tom rescues Buffy from the attentions of a drunk; walking outside with him Buffy finds broken glass on the ground and sees the boarded up second floor window. Xander, who has gatecrashed the party is caught, and the brothers begin to haze him.

Investigating the bracelet, Willow and Giles discover that Callie Megan Anderson is missing from Kent Preparatory School. Meanwhile a drugged Buffy collapses on a bed at the frat house, with Cordelia on the floor nearby. Tom stops another frat brother interfering with Buffy, saying that she is there *"for the pleasure of the one we serve."*

Finding that two other girls went missing a year ago almost to the day, Giles and Willow call Angel. As they go to the frat house, Willow has to tell them that Buffy is at the party there. Buffy, Cordelia and Callie are chained to a wall in the basement of the frat house; Tom tells them they are offerings to Machida, Machida being a half-man half-snake demon who chooses this opportune moment to emerge from a well in the basement and view his 'offerings.'

Willow, Giles, and Angel find Xander wearing fraternity robes (to cover his nakedness—the result of his hazing). Xander uses his robes to get into the house, but by the time they reach the basement Buffy has broken free. As she beats up Tom and dispatches Machida, a fight breaks out with the rest of the brothers. At the end of the episode the fraternity brothers are headed jailward, corporations whose chairmen and founders are former Delta Zeta Kappas are suffering from falling profits, IRS raids and suicides in the boardroom.

And Buffy agrees to go out for coffee with Angel... some time.

## Halloween (10/27/97), Episode:5V06

Written by Carl Ellsworth, Directed by Bruce Seth Green.

While Buffy is slaying a vampire in Pop's Pumpkin Patch she is being secretly videotaped for Spike by a vampire in the shadows. Late, and severely ruffled, for a date at the Bronze with Angel, she arrives to find he has been intercepted by Cordelia, and they seem to be getting on fine. Angel tries to reassure her, but Buffy, hair full of hay, is feeling down and leaves.

Volunteered by Principal Snyder for a Halloween safety program to oversee a group of trick-or-treating children for two hours on Halloween, Buffy is distinctly underwhelmed. Xander defends Buffy's honour to school jock Larry (whose secret will emerge in *Phases*). About to fight, he is saved by Buffy, who has unwittingly *"violated the guy code big time."* Buffy and Willow 'borrow' Watcher diaries from Giles' office in order to learn more about Angel, and find in them a drawing of an

18th-century noblewoman who Buffy thinks is Angel's type. Ethan, the costume shop owner (a suave Brit) convinces Buffy to buy a beautiful 18th-century gown for Halloween. Watching the videotape of Buffy in action, Spike is trying to work out how to kill her. Drusilla predicts that something is going to happen on Halloween night, because someone has come to change it. We find the costume shop owner conducting a candlelit ritual before a bust of the Roman god Janus, saying, *"Chaos, I remain, as ever, thy faithful, degenerate son."*

Willow can't be persuaded to wear a sexy, revealing outfit for Halloween—she puts a white sheet ghost costume on over it. Willow joins Buffy and Xander in taking the kids out trick-or-treating, and as the ritual takes effect, everyone becomes the literal embodiment of their costumes. Willow finds she's a real ghost, Xander has become a tough soldier and when they find Buffy she faints, having become an 18th-century noblewoman.

Buffy and Xander don't remember who they are, so Willow gets them back to Buffy's house, where they find Angel and Cordelia, who (despite wearing a costume) is unchanged. Willow leaves Xander in charge while she goes to the library. Angel defends Buffy from a demon, becoming his vampiric self as he does so. This scares Buffy, who runs away. Willow and Giles realise everyone but Cordelia got their costumes from Ethan's. Spike overhears Angel saying that Buffy's out there and he leads a troupe of demons to find her first.

Running into trouble with Larry, Buffy is saved by Xander, who finds a *"weird sense of closure"* in dealing with him. Ethan is Ethan Rayne, an old acquaintance of Giles who derides Giles' Watcher act. *"They have no idea where you come from,"* he insinuates. Giles coldly beats Ethan until he tells him how to break the spell. Spike has caught up with Buffy, but just as he is about to deliver the *coup de grace*, Giles breaks the spell, and Buffy is back. With his demon army reverting to kids and Buffy delivering a king-sized kicking, Spike legs it, and Buffy goes home with Angel. Willow wakes up where her corporeal body was left. She tosses her ghost outfit and walks home in her sexy outfit, getting an appreciative stare from Oz.

The next day, Giles returns to Ethan's store, which is bare except for a note saying, *'Be seeing you.'*

## Lie To Me (11/03/97), Episode:5V07

Written & Directed by Joss Whedon.

Buffy sees Angel talking to Drusilla at the cemetery. Catching a misleading end to their conversation, she is struck by a fit of jealousy. The next day at school an old friend, Billy 'Ford' Fordham, has transferred to Sunnydale from their old school. Ford tells her he knows she's the Slayer, but later on he goes to the Sunset Club. As he enters we can hear a Sisters of Mercy tune playing—a pretty good clue we're in Gothville.

Angel feels something wrong about Ford, and enlists Willow's help in investigating him. As Buffy and Ford fight some vampires who are on school grounds, Ford tells one of them he'll spare her if she tells him what he wants to know, and later tells Buffy that he killed her. Angel, Willow and Xander go to the Sunset Club—the only address they can find for Ford. It's full of wannabe vampires. Concerned about two vampires coming onto campus, Buffy pages Giles, rescuing him from a Monster Trucks rally with Jenny Calendar. Buffy identifies Drusilla in one of Giles' books, and as Giles looks for further information, the girl vampire that Ford said he'd killed appears, takes a book, and escapes. At Spike's lair Ford offers Spike Buffy in exchange for making him a vampire. Spike agrees, despite his obvious contempt for Ford.

When Angel warns Buffy about Ford she asks him about Drusilla. Angel tells her that he created Drusilla out of obsession. She was pure and he made her insane by killing everybody she loved and, when she fled to a convent, he turned her into a demon on the day she took her holy orders.

Buffy meets Ford at the Sunset Club, where Ford and friends trap her inside. They think that they're going to live forever like 'the lonely ones.' she explains that to Spike they'll just be an *"all-you-can-eat moron bar."* Ford knows his friends will die, but he has only six months to live—for him it's his last chance.

Cometh the sunset, cometh the Spike, who issues the order to *"save the Slayer for me."* And chows down on Chantarelle (who will reappear in *Anne,* season three). Buffy saves Chantarelle from Spike and holds Drusilla hostage, telling Spike to *"let everyone out, or your girlfriend fits in an ashtray."* Buffy and the children of Anne Rice are released, leaving Ford inside with Spike.

The next day Buffy returns to the Sunset Club and finds Ford's dead body. At the cemetery she has tears in her eyes as she lays a wreath on his grave. She talks to Giles about the problems of right and wrong, good and evil. Ford rises from the grave and she plunges a stake into his heart.

*The Verdict:* Any Anne Rice fan will recognise the misplaced enthusiasms and the costumery of the wannabe vampires in this episode. It's almost a perverse re-working of *Interview With The Vampire,* with Ford's very real and desperate need to be a vampire contrasted with his friends naïve, romantic view of the process.

## The Dark Age (11/10/97), Episode:5V08

Written by Dean Batali & Rob Des Hotel, Directed by Bruce Seth Green.

Wandering Sunnydale High campus at night, looking for Rupert Giles, a man gets as far as the library door, where a decaying corpse he calls Dierdre kills him and turns into greenish slime, which spreads into his body.

After a night filled with bad dreams Giles reminds Buffy that they have to monitor a delivery of blood to the hospital for possible vampiric activity. A romantic interlude with Jenny Calendar is interrupted when the police want him to look at a man found dead outside the library with Giles' name and address in his pocket. Giles identifies the man as Philip Henry, an old friend he hasn't seen in twenty years, and tells them he doesn't know the meaning of the tattoo on Phillip's arm. Buffy stops the vampires at the hospital with Angel's help when Giles doesn't appear. Giles comes to his door looking tired, awful, a tad drunk, and dismisses Buffy. On the phone Giles discovers that Dierdre Page has died recently. He looks at a tattoo on his arm— one identical to Philip's. At the morgue, Philip's corpse reanimates…

Xander, Cordelia and Willow's Saturday computer lesson with Jenny Calendar is interrupted by Buffy, concerned by Giles' behaviour. Cordelia tells her about the police and Buffy goes to the library where she is attacked by Ethan Rayne (*Halloween*). Restraining him she wakes Giles from further bad dreams by calling him, demanding to know what the 'Mark of Eyghon' is. Philip's corpse arrives trying to kill Ethan and Buffy locks Phillip in the book cage. Giles arrives and efficiently roughs up Ethan, who taunts him for putting his friends in danger. Philip escapes, and Jenny Calendar is knocked unconscious as Buffy overpowers

Philip, who dissolves into slime, which touches Jenny's hand. Regaining consciousness Jenny hugs Giles for comfort.

Willow, Xander and Cordelia find that Eyghon, a demon, can only exist in this reality by possessing an unconscious host. If the possession isn't undone, it becomes permanent and Eyghon is 'born from within the host.' They realise that Jenny Calendar must be possessed.

At Giles' house, Jenny Calendar becomes sexually aggressive to Giles, becoming demonic and attacking him. Buffy saves him and finally Giles tells her that as a young man he fell in with bad crowd, who summoned Eyghon for the high. One of them, Randall, had to have Eyghon exorcised, which killed him. They thought they were free, but now only Giles and Ethan remain. Buffy goes to Ethan's costume shop to protect him, but he knocks her unconscious, tattoos her with the mark of Eyghon, and removes his own tattoo with acid. Jenny Calendar appears at the shop and fights Buffy. Willow brings Angel to the shop, who attacks Eyghon. Under threat the demon transfers into the nearest dead host: Angel, whose demon fights and destroys Eyghon. Ethan has vanished.

Jenny Calendar, unnerved by her experience, doesn't want Giles to touch her. Buffy tells Giles that she's used to him being a grownup, and is surprised to find out that he's a person.

*The Verdict: Casting of the Runes*, anyone? Another Buffy remake of a classic horror subject (best known as the Jacques Tourneur film *Night of the Demon*), done with style and verve.

## What's My Line (Part 1) (11/17/97), Episode:5V09

Written by Howard Gordon & Marti Noxon, Directed by David Solomon

It's Career Week at Sunnydale High, Slayers need not apply—their fate is sealed, and Buffy is down. The book that was stolen from Giles in *Lie To Me* turns out to be a key part of Spike's plan to restore Drusilla to strength; only one problem—the book is in code. On patrol Buffy sees Dalton, the vampire who is trying to decode the book for Spike, and another vampire looting a mausoleum—she's able to kill one of them but Dalton escapes with something. Returning home, Angel is there to add to the cheer by telling her he 'had a bad feeling'. Buffy tells him of her childhood dreams of wanting to be ice skater Dorothy Hamill, and they make a date to go skating the next day.

Giles is worried about what was taken from the mausoleum. Spike now has part of Drusilla's cure, but he realises he'll never complete it with a Slayer breathing down his neck and decides to employ bounty hunters to take care of her. Giles and Buffy examine the mausoleum and Giles realises its occupant was Josephus du Lac—the author of the stolen book, a book of evil spells. Something has been stolen from his crypt, and it's a good bet it's not good news.

Strangers start hitting town; a door-to-door cosmetic salesman, a guy who looks like a refugee from WWF and a beautiful black woman, who knocks an airport employee unconscious before emerging from the hold of a plane.

Buffy has her skate-date with Angel, and is attacked by the Undertaker's uglier brother, who is dispatched when she cuts his throat with her skate blade. They are being watched by the beautiful woman. Angel recognises the killer's ring, and Giles identifies it as the symbol of the Order of Taraka—supernatural bounty hunters who'll stop at nothing to kill everything in their paths. Buffy hides at Angel's apartment as Angel looks for information about Order of Taraka. In a local bar, Angel is attacked by the beautiful woman, who locks him in a cage where he'll be killed by sunlight within hours. Spike finds the answer to curing Drusilla. Xander and Cordelia look for Buffy at her house and Cordelia lets the cosmetics salesman in... At Angel's apartment, Buffy is attacked by the beautiful woman with an axe. They fight each other to a stalemate. When Buffy asks the girl who she is, she responds with *"I am Kendra, the Vampire Slayer."*

*To be continued...*

Quote of the show:

Dalton: *"Uh, yes, but... The Order of Taraka, I mean... isn't that overkill?"*

Spike: *"No, I think it's just about enough kill."*

## What's My Line (Part 2) (11/24/97), Episode:5V10

Written by Marti Noxon, Directed by David Semel.

Buffy realises that Kendra was summoned as the new Slayer when she temporarily died in *Prophecy Girl*. Kendra has been told by her Watcher that evil is coming in Sunnydale and has been sent to fight it. Nearly dead at daybreak Angel is turned over to Spike and Drusilla by Willy, the bar owner—they need the blood of her sire to revive Drusilla. At the new moon that night, they will perform the ritual from the stolen book and Angel will die.

Buffy wonders whether she should let Kendra be the Slayer, and have a normal life. At Buffy's house, Cordelia chats to the cosmetics salesman, until she realises he has bugs on him—in fact he's composed of mealworms. As he changes into a mass of them Cordelia and Xander flee and barricade themselves in the basement, where they fight, and, as the argument heightens, kiss passionately. Finally they escape and drive off in Cordelia's car. At Sunnydale High, Willow talks to Oz about their similar Career Fair paths when a police woman supervising the fair opens fire on Buffy and accidentally shoots Oz, Kendra coming to Buffy's rescue. Giles tells everyone that Angel will die that night in the ritual to revive Drusilla—it'll take place in a church. But which of the forty-three in Sunnydale will it be? Buffy and Kendra go to the bar to find Angel, but Kendra leaves, apparently convinced that Angel is evil. Drusilla is torturing Angel by dousing him with holy water and watching him writhe in pain.

Drusilla: *"Say 'Uncle'. Oh, that's right, you killed my uncle."*

Willy leads Buffy to the church where Spike is carrying out the ritual, where she is trapped by vampires and Tarakan assassins. Buffy watches in horror as Drusilla, connected to Angel by a blade stabbed through their hands, saps his power. Spike instructs the policewoman assassin to shoot Buffy, but Kendra enters and saves her. Willow, Xander, Cordelia and Giles arrive; Kendra leaving Buffy alone was a ruse so they could track her to the right church. Spike is not best pleased with Willy over this. Xander and Cordelia wait for the cosmetics salesman to turn into bugs, pour glue over the bugs and stamp on them. As Buffy releases Angel, Spike sets the room on fire and grabs Drusilla. Before they can escape, Buffy hurls the censer from the altar at them, literally bringing the house down on them.

The next day, Oz charms Willow; Xander and Cordelia again argue passionately and kiss passionately, and Buffy says goodbye to Kendra, who tells her that Slaying isn't a job. *"It's who you are."*

In the church the fire has burnt itself out. Drusilla emerges from the rubble now restored to full strength, carrying the injured

Spike to safety.

Drusilla: *"Don't worry, dear heart. I'll see that you get strong again. Like me!"*

*The Verdict:* An excellent two-parter that redefines a lot of relationships: Willow and Oz, Spike and Drusilla, Xander and Cordelia and even Buffy and Angel as she becomes the rescuer for the first time.

*Continuity:* In *Never Kill a Boy on the First Date,* Giles tells us that there's no instruction manual, but in this episode we find out there is a Slayer Handbook. This seems to rival the Junior Woodchucks Manual held by Huey Dewey and Louie in Carl Barks' Donald Duck oeuvre for complexity and completeness and one wonders if this is an in-joke.

## Ted (12/08/97), Episode:5V11

Written by David Greenwalt & Joss Whedon, Directed by Bruce Seth Green.

Buffy's mom Joyce's new boyfriend, Ted cooks and he's a computer specialist—making him an instant hit with Xander and Willow, although Buffy obviously doesn't take to him. At school, Giles awkwardly chats with Jenny Calendar, but his concern about her well-being is getting on her nerves. Ted invites everyone out for a game of miniature golf, where his remarks about Buffy's grades and his constant reference to her as 'little lady' grates. He talks to Buffy alone and reveals a decidedly psychotic side to his nature, thumping his golf club repeatedly against his leg and threatening to hit her.

Suspicious, Buffy visits the company where Ted sells computers. He's known as 'the Machine,' and it's common knowledge there that Ted plans to marry Joyce in two months. When Buffy raises this at home that night she gets sent to her room for her troubles. She sneaks to go on patrol and when she climbs back in her window she finds Ted sitting in her room. He's gone through her things and read her diary. He threatens to show the diary to Buffy's mother if she doesn't stop trying to cause trouble. When Buffy tries to take the diary back, they fight and Buffy knocks him down the stairs, apparently killing him.

Buffy goes to school consumed with guilt and remorse for killing a human being. Xander, Willow and Cordelia start investigating to try to help Buffy deal with the trauma. When

Xander goes from being extremely concerned to laid back Willow realises that Xander's change of attitude coincides with him eating one of Ted's homebaked cookies. Analysis shows the cookies contain a tranquilliser. Cordelia discovers that Ted has had four wives...

At the cemetery Jenny and Giles resolve their conflicts in time for a vampire to attack Giles, and Jenny to shoot Giles (instead of the vampire) with the crossbow. Giles removes the bow and kills the vampire.

Ted arrives, distinctly undead (well, not dead, if you see what I mean), in Buffy's room. He attacks her and stabbing him with a nail file she discovers he's a robot. Xander, Willow and Cordelia go to his house and find what's left of Ted's ex-wives in his closet. Fighting an electronic stutter, Ted knocks Buffy unconscious, and goes downstairs to see Joyce, telling her that he was dead for six minutes but then revived. He tries to get her to leave with him; even the dense Joyce can spot that something's wrong. He knocks her out and as he's about to leave with her he hears Buffy. Going to take care of her, Buffy takes care of him instead, dispatching him with a blow from a skillet. They find that the original Ted was a man whose wife left him, so he built a robotic version of himself who kept trying to bring back his wife. Ted is dismantled, and Giles is reconciled with Ms Calendar.

At school, Buffy and Willow look into the library through the round door windows and immediately turn around and leave. Inside the library Giles and Jenny are making out.

*The Verdict:* Another *Buffy* remake (*The Stepford Wives* in reverse) enlivened by a first rate performance from John Ritter as Ted.

### Bad Eggs (01/12/98), Episode:5V12

Written by Marti Noxon, Directed by David Greenwalt.

At the Mall Buffy fights with a cowboy vampire who exits with the line 'This ain't over!' In the excitement she's forgotten to pick up a dress for her mother. *"A little responsibility is all I ask,"* says the Whiny One. The next day Mr Whitmore, the teen health teacher, gives the class eggs to watch over as though they were babies, as a lesson in the *"number one negative consequence of sexual activity."*

Buffy gets Angel's help looking for Lyle and Tector Gorch, who Giles has identified as cowboy vampire brothers, but they wind up kissing, observe by the Gorches. As she sleeps that night, a tentacle emerges from the egg Buffy's placed by her bedside and rests on her face.

The following day Mr Whitmore doesn't show up for school and Buffy and Willow are both sluggish. Xander has hard-boiled his egg, as a protection against damage. That night a security guard discovers that the door to Sunnydale High's basement is open and there is huge hole in the basement wall. Mr Whitmore appears from behind the guard and pushes him into the hole.

Buffy returns home late after being on patrol to find her egg twitching. It breaks open, and a small, multi-legged creature springs out and attacks her, alien style. She kills it and calls Willow to warn her, but Willow says her egg is normal. We see that Willow's egg has in fact hatched. The noise of Buffy killing the creature has wakened her mother, who, finding Buffy dressed at that late hour, grounds her for eternity.

Buffy tells Giles about the creature by phone, and asks the rest about their eggs. Cordelia says hers is OK, but Xander tries to eat his, and finds a boiled creature inside it. Willow suggests they take it to the science lab to dissect—we see that one of the creatures is attached to Willow's lower back. As they start to dissect it Willow tells them *"It's possible that Mr Whitmore wasn't harmed. Maybe the offspring simply used him to return to the mother bezoar."* Willow and Cordelia promptly knock Buffy and Xander out and lock them in a closet, then join a posse of other students with shovels and picks on a trip to the basement. Joyce arrives to pick up the grounded Buffy, but finds Giles, who makes small talk and then puts one of the creatures on her neck. Joyce is added to the basement team.

Buffy and Xander escape from the closet and find Giles' research: the bezoar is a pre-prehistoric parasite who takes control of its victims' motor functions. They find the possessed students in the basement digging up the mother bezoar. The Gorch brothers show up and Buffy and Lyle fight, while Tector gets eaten by the mother. Lyle dazes Buffy long enough for her to be dragged down by the mother, grabbing a pick as she does so. Audible beating noises ensure, ending in Buffy emerging from the pit containing the dead mother, covered in black slime. Lyle takes one look at her and legs it, saying 'It's over!' as he goes. The possession is broken, with Giles leading everyone to believe it was a gas leak. The incredibly unobservant Joyce confines Buffy to her room, where she is forced to make out with Angel—on a ladder outside her house.

*The Verdict: Alien* meets *Invasion of the Body Snatchers* anyone? A definite filler episode with too much kissy-face between Buffy and Angel and far too much of Joyce Summers.

## Surprise (01/19/98), Episode:5V13

Written by Marti Noxon, Directed by Michael Lange.

Buffy is plagued by a dream in which Drusilla stakes Angel, who disintegrates as she reaches him. *"Happy birthday, Buffy,"* Drusilla says. At school, having checked Angel's OK Buffy tells Willow she wants to have sex with Angel. Willow invites Oz to Buffy's seventeenth birthday surprise party the following night for. Telling Giles about her dream Buffy confesses she's worried that Drusilla is still alive. A worry she's right to have: Drusilla and Spike are alive, though Spike is burned and confined to a wheelchair. Drusilla is also arranging a party, which seems to involve a lot of wooden boxes.

Buffy's birthday day starts with a bad omen when Joyce acts out part of Buffy's nightmare. Jenny Calendar has a visitor who reprimands her for neglecting her gypsy heritage. The elder woman of the tribe can see that Angel's torment is lessening. We find that the visitor is Jenny's uncle and she promises him that she'll end Buffy and Angel's relationship. That night, taking Buffy to the Bronze for what we know is her surprise party, they're journey is interrupted by the necessity to intercept a crew of vampires with more of the wooden boxes we've see with Drusilla. Buffy fights with them, bursting into the Bronze and her surprise party. She carries one of the boxes inside, and opens it to find an armour-clad arm — which leaps from the box and starts to strangle her.

Angel gets the arm off Buffy, and tells them that it's part of the Judge, a demon brought forth to rid the Earth of the plague of humanity.

The Judge can't be killed, so was dismembered and the pieces scattered in every corner of the earth. Jenny Calendar suggests Angel is the only one who can take the arm and re-bury it; Angel agrees, despite Buffy's protests. As Buffy and Angel part at the docks they're attacked by vampires, who regain the arm. The Judge is at last reassembled.

Drusilla: *"He's perfect, my darling. Just what I wanted."*

Buffy and Angel are too late to stop the Judge from being reassembled, and are caught by Spike and Drusilla. They escape and return to Angel's apartment, they kiss and the inevitable happens. Waking up with a sudden start in bed with Buffy, Angel gets up and rushes off. Outside in the alley Angel crashes through the door into the rain, and falls to the ground. He cries out in pain.

Angel: *'Buffy!'*

Buffy sleeps on...

*To be continued...*

## Innocence (01/20/98), Episode:5V14

Written & Directed by Joss Whedon.

The Judge sits waiting, impervious to Spike's impatience, when Drusilla collapses, moaning Angel's name. Buffy awakens in Angel's bed, but he's gone. Angel is outside in the rainswept alley, convulsing in pain. A hooker asks him if he wants her to call an 911. 'No,' he says, 'the pain is gone,' and spins around, grabs her and violently bites her on the neck to feed. Angelus is back.

Buffy reports that the Judge has been reassembled; she's worried because Angel hasn't been heard from. Angel appears at Spike and Drusilla's; when The Judge tells them that there is no humanity in him, they realise that Angelus has returned. They tell him they're going to destroy the world, but he just wants to kill Buffy.

Angelus: *"She made me feel like a human being. That's not the kind of thing you just forgive."*

Willow surprises Xander and Cordelia kissing and runs from the library disgusted.

Xander: *"Willow, we were just kissing. It doesn't mean that much."*

Willow: *"No. It just means that you'd rather be with someone you hate than be with me."*

Buffy looks for Angel at his apartment, but when she finds him he taunts her, implying that their night together was just a one-night stand, of little consequence. Jenny's uncle explains that if Angel found even one moment of true happiness and contentment his soul would once again leave him. Angelus appears at the school and tempts Willow to come to him; Jenny tells Willow that he's not Angel anymore. Jenny is holding a cross up to him, which Xander takes and shoves into Angelus from behind, making him leave.

As they try to work out what turned Angel back to Angelus, Buffy realises and runs from the library in tears; Willow also realises what must have happened. Gloating about tormenting Buffy to Spike and Drusilla, Angelus is beginning to annoy Spike.

Buffy removes the claddagh ring Angel gave her and cries herself to sleep. She dreams of a funeral, where Angel says *"You have to know what to see,"* followed by Jenny Calendar lifting a veil from her face. To Giles' dismay Jenny admits that she was sent to keep Buffy and Angel apart, but that she didn't know what would happen.

Oz drives Willow, Xander and Cordelia to the Sunnydale army base. There, using the knowledge he retained from his time as a soldier in *Halloween*, Xander gets into the armoury. Jenny Calendar takes Giles and Buffy to her uncle, who they find dead, killed by Angelus. Buffy knows she has to kill Angelus.

Angelus and Drusilla take The Judge to start the massacre, leaving the wheelchair-bound Spike behind. Oz figures out where the massacre will be: the mall. At the mall, the Judge begins to suck the life from the patrons, but gets a wake-up call in the form of a crossbow bolt from Buffy.

Judge: *"You're a fool. No weapon forged can stop me."*

Buffy: *"That was then. This is now."*

She shoulders the rocket launcher they've stolen from the armoury and blows the Judge to bits. While the others pick up the Judge's pieces, she fights Angelus, but finds she can't stake him. She kicks him in the groin, doubling him over in pain.

Buffy: *'Give me time.'*

Buffy and Joyce share a quiet birthday celebration. *"So what did you do for your birthday? Did you have fun?"* her mother asks. 'I got older,' Buffy replies.

*The Verdict:* A superb and series defining two parter, with both Gellar and Boreanaz showing acting abilities you didn't know they had, and a benchmark for the series to this point.

## Phases (01/27/98), Episode:5V15

Written by Rob Des Hotel & Dean Batali, Directed by Bruce Seth Green.

Willow is discussing Oz with Buffy—he hasn't tried to kiss her yet, although she's happy he's being so respectful. Xander and Cordelia are parked in the woods, making out in her soft-top sports car. A large hairy arm shoots through the soft-top, interrupting the lovers. Cordelia puts the car into reverse dislodging the excitable and hirsute creature from the top of the car and drives off as fast as she can.

Xander is convinced that they have encountered a werewolf, thrilling Giles who has never encountered one before. Buffy's gym class is studying self-defence, but Buffy's pretence of normality is put at risk when an obnoxious sexist jock named Larry uses this as an excuse to 'grab' her. Buffy throws Larry across the room. Theresa, a classmate of Buffy is walking home when she seems to sense someone following her. She checks behind her, and turning back encounters Angelus who says he'll walk her home.

Buffy and Giles are staking out Lover's Lane for the werewolf when Buffy is ensnared by a net that lifts her off the ground. The net is the work of a werewolf hunter called Cain, who now appears with a shotgun. After cutting Buffy down, Cain explains he hunts werewolves for money. Buffy and Giles are disgusted by his attitude to a creature that is human twenty-seven days of the month and when he asks them about local teenager hangouts (werewolves are attracted by sexual activity, you see) they feign ignorance.

Pretty obviously Sunnydale's all-purpose teen nightspot (which given the mayhem regularly enacted there should have been closed by now) is the place to be. As Buffy and Giles arrive dozens of frightened teenagers are running from the club—the werewolf is already inside. Buffy has a chain fight with the werewolf, and ties it up, but it is too powerful, breaks free and escapes.

Enter cheesed-off Cain who can't believe that Buffy tried to capture it instead of kill it, and points out that any deaths it causes will be on her head. Meanwhile our werewolf chum discovers Theresa's body (you didn't really think Angelus was taking her home, did you?). Looking up, the werewolf sees Angelus.

Buffy and Giles hear about Theresa and instantly assume it was the werewolf. They have only one night left before the werewolf becomes fully human for the rest of the month.

We see the werewolf sleeping, and as the sun rises, it reverts to its human form. In one of the less surprising moments of the series, we see that the werewolf is Oz. Oz is beginning to suspect that waking naked in the woods is not normal behaviour, and contacts his Aunt about his cousin Jordy, who bit him recently. She confirms that Jordy is a werewolf, and hey, now so is Oz! Oz has a less than good day at school, not least when he learns he may have killed Theresa.

Xander, suspecting the over-hormoned Larry may be the werewolf, confronts him in the locker room. Unfortunately Larry is *not* the werewolf but *is* gay, and (in one of the funniest scenes in the series) assumes that the 'secret' that Xander is talking about is this. The scene ends with Larry believing that Xander is also gay and feeling that he will no longer have to pretend to be so sexually aggressive towards women to cover his true nature.

Buffy and Xander finally get up the wits to check whether Theresa was really killed by a werewolf. The matter is resolved swiftly when Theresa is reborn as a vampire, telling Buffy that Angel sent her. Xander is forced to stake her through the back while Buffy is plainly unnerved by this knowledge.

Oz is busily attempting self-bondage with a box of chains and shackles when Willow arrives, upset by his decision to stay home instead of spending the time with her. Oz tries persuade her to leave (cue another misunderstanding about the nature of the 'changes' Oz is going through) but his transformation has already begun. Willow runs screaming from the house, chased by werewolf. Intelligently she ends up in the woods (?) but before the werewolf can attack her he catches a different scent (unfortunately it's Cain's) and leaves Willow alone. Willow runs to the library and tells Giles and Buffy that Oz is the werewolf. They arrive at the woods just in time for Buffy to kick the shotgun from Cain's hand and fight the werewolf. Giles tries to get a clean shot at the werewolf with his tranquilliser gun, but it is knocked from his hands by a flying Buffy. Willow grabs the tranquilliser gun and shoots the charging werewolf. Cain is given his marching orders when Buffy turns his gun into an attractive pretzel shape with her bare hands, then orders him to leave.

To Oz's surprise Willow wants to continue their relationship—Oz will be fine as long as he does the chains and locks thing around the full moon. As she leaves, Willow kisses Oz for the first time.

*The Verdict:* Another in the line of monster movie remakes that Buffy goes in for every so long. Efficiently done and amusing in parts, this is not a top rate episode, and the addition of Oz to the collection of supernatural friends and foes is worrying—every new cast member shouldn't have to have a dark past/supernatural power.

## Bewitched, Bothered and Bewildered (02/10/98), Episode:5V16

Written by Marti Noxon, Directed by James A. Contner.

Xander plans to give Cordelia a silver heart necklace at the upcoming Valentine's Day dance to legitimise their relationship. After Angel, Buffy plans to spend Valentine's Day with her mother.

Cordelia is ostracised by her friends, who know she's been seeing Xander. Xander sees Amy (from *Witch*) work some sort of witchcraft on Miss Beakman. Giles is avoiding Jenny Calendar. He tells Buffy that Angelus performs particularly evil acts around Valentine's Day, and asks her to stay in for a few nights. Angel is both considering ways to 'show his regard' for Buffy, and is being over attentive to Drusilla, aggravating the wheelchair-bound Spike.

Xander gives Cordelia the heart necklace at the dance, to find her breaking up with him. When he finds that everyone at school knows he's been dumped he blackmails Amy to cast a love spell on Cordelia for him as revenge.

Xander demands the necklace back from Cordelia to provide the personal object Amy needs to cast a love spell, and the spell is cast that night. Cordelia is as snotty as ever to Xander; however in the library he finds Buffy and Amy fighting over him. Rushing home, he finds Willow in his bed and he runs away to explain his problem to Giles. The library ends in a free-for-all with Jenny Calendar, Buffy and Amy fighting over Xander, ending with Amy turning Buffy into a rat.

The love spell has affected every woman in Sunnydale *except* Cordelia, who is attacked by her former friends for dumping their now beloved Xander. Oz volunteers to help catch the Buffy-rat and Giles, disgusted with Xander, sends him home. On the way he saves Cordelia from the mob, only to run into a second mob, led by an axe-wielding Willow. The two groups clash and Xander and Cordelia run to Buffy's house, where Joyce lets them in, but soon starts to make advances to Xander. Cordelia locks Joyce outside and goes to Buffy's room—where Angelus promptly pulls Xander out the window, planning to kill him as a Valentine's Day gift for Buffy. Ironically a Xander-besotted Drusilla appears and saves him, but wants to make him into a vampire! The mobs converge on Buffy's house, and Cordelia and Xander barricade themselves in the basement. As the mob breaks in Cordelia realises that the spell was meant for her. Oz has tracked the Buffy-rat to the school's basement and as it nears a mousetrap, and the mob has Xander and Cordelia pinned in Buffy's basement, Giles and Amy break the spell. Oz is left with a naked Buffy, and Cordelia has to convince the bewildered women that it was a scavenger hunt. all Everything is (relatively) normal in Sunnydale again, although Willow won't speak to Xander. Cordelia stands up to her friends, claiming Xander as her man, *"no matter how lame he is!"*

### Passion (02/24/98), Episode:5V17

Written by Ty King, Directed by Michael E. Gershman.

Angelus narrates this episode.

Buffy wakes to find a sketch of her sleeping face, and knows that Angelus has been in her bedroom while she sleeps. Buffy asks Giles to find a spell to negate the invitation into her home. They both stop by Jenny Calendar's computer class to meet Willow, who Jenny has assigned as fill class teacher the next day. Jenny tries to apologise to Giles, who tells her that Buffy is the one who deserves the apology. She confesses that she loves Giles, and gives him a book she thinks will be helpful to him.

Buffy tells her mother that Angelus has been stalking her, and that Joyce should never invite him into the house. Willow discovers that all the fish from her aquarium have been removed and strung along a wire, placed in an envelope on her bed. Willow goes to Buffy's house to spend the night.

Spike is growing increasingly tired of Angelus, and their argument is interrupted by Drusilla who senses something that may endanger them. This is Jenny Calendar's purchase of an Orb of Thesulah, which she needs to restore Angelus's soul. Jenny is working on a computer program that could translate the necessary text.

Giles gives Jenny's book to Buffy; it contains a revoking spell, which they first perform on Cordelia's car, then on Willow's house, where they find a sketch of Joyce, asleep. Angelus intercepts Joyce at the house where he pleads with her to help him get Buffy back, mentioning that they have made love. Angelus tries to follow Joyce into the house but is held back by a force. He sees Buffy and Willow coming down the stairs—they have performed the revoking spell. Jenny tells Giles she may have some good news, and he invites her to stop by his house later. Jenny completes her program and saves the translated text on a floppy disk. As she prints the text Angelus arrives and destroys the Orb of Thesulah, her computer, and the printout, finally snapping her neck.

Giles returns home to music playing and a rose on his door. He enters and a romantic scene—music, flowers and note that reads 'Upstairs'. He goes upstairs, to where Jenny's dead body lies in his bed. Before going to the police station Giles rings Buffy. Angelus watches through the windows as Willow takes the phone from Buffy and Buffy slowly slides down the wall into a crouch. Willow immediately bursts into tears.

Giles takes off, as Buffy and the others arrive too late. At Spike's Giles throws a Molotov cocktail setting the place ablaze. Drusilla runs away with Spike wheeling right behind her. Angelus is hit in the shoulder with a crossbow bolt. Giles walks toward him with a baseball bat, which he puts into the flames, and it catches fire. He swings it and hits Angelus in the face,. Finally, Angelus grabs Giles by the neck and picks him up, but Buffy arrives. Their battle carries on to the catwalk above, but before Buffy can finish Angelus off, he reminds her of Giles, collapsed by the rapidly spreading flames. Buffy rescues Giles, thus allowing to Angelus to escape once again. Outside, Giles rails at Buffy for interfering in his fight, but she punches him to the ground, begins to cry and crouches down to hug him.

Buffy: *"You can't leave me. I can't do this alone."*

Giles and Buffy stand over Jenny's grave. In the computer classroom, Willow takes over as substitute teacher until the new teacher arrives. Arranging Jenny's desk, she unknowingly knocks the disk with the transcribed spell on it between the desk and the small filing cabinet.

There the disk lies, the key to Angel's restoration.

### Killed By Death (03/03/98), Episode:5V18

Written by Rob Des Hotel & Dean Batali, Directed by Deran Sarafian.

Buffy is on patrol suffering from a flu bug that's taken half the student body of Sunnydale High out of school. She fights Angelus but weakly, and Angelus has her at his mercy until the others drive him off with crosses. Buffy then collapses.

At the hospital a delirious Buffy is not happy about staying. Delirious she yells about vampires, until sedated. Joyce explains Buffy has hated hospitals since she saw her beloved cousin Celia die in one when she was eight. Willow and Xander worry that Angelus can get into the hospital. Buffy wakes up delirious with fever, and sees a young boy at her door, who leaves followed by a grotesque humanoid figure dressed in black. She tries to follow but she wakes up again in her bed. She goes to the children's ward, where she sees a dead girl being wheeled away, and hears Dr. Wilkinson argue with a doctor named Backer about his controversial methods. The young boy she saw, Ryan, tells her, *"He comes at night. The grown-ups don't see him. He was with Tina. He'll come back for us."*

The next day. Wilkinson tells Buffy the fever's gone down and is amazed by her fast recovery. Giles and her friends arrive, and she tells them about the previous night. Xander and Cordelia go through the hospital's files to see what killed Tina. Buffy visits the children's ward, where Ryan is drawing a picture of the creature he calls Death. Willow and Giles think the children are afraid of a real person, possibly Dr. Backer, who has a record of unauthorised experimentation. Dr. Backer seems to have a breakthrough, and goes to the children's ward to test it, where he is attacked by an invisible creature. When Buffy tries to help, the creature hits her and drags Dr. Backer's body away.

Buffy gives Ryan's picture to Giles. In Dr. Backer's office, Willow and Buffy discover that his work was legitimate, and had been helping the children. Cordelia and Giles discover the creature's identity; *Der Kindestod*—literally 'child death'. Buffy realises that her cousin Celia was killed by the Kindestod. She realises that her fever allowed her to see it, so Willow re-infects her. They find the children's ward empty—the kids are heading to the basement. As Buffy watches, the Kindestod appears and follows them. She fights the Kindestod in the basement, and eventually reaches up and snaps his neck. Buffy returns home, where she receives a curiously gruesome drawing from a grateful Ryan. It's of Buffy standing over the Kindestod with her foot up on its chest. The monster's neck is split open and blood is gushing out.

## I Only Have Eyes For You (04/28/98), Episode:5V19

Written by Marti Noxon, Directed by James Whitmore Jr.

At the Bronze Buffy is asked out to the Sadie Hawkins dance by a boy and turns him down on the basis she's not seeing anyone *"Ever again, actually."* Willow tries persuade her she should look for life after Angelus, but Buffy goes to see if Giles needs her. In one of the school hallways an apparently peaceful couple start to fight. The boy holds a gun as the girl tries to leave the scene. Buffy arrives at the school just in time to knock the gun from his hand, and he returns to his senses. He and the girl tell Buffy that they don't know why they were arguing and the school janitor notices that the gun has disappeared.

Principal Snyder calls Buffy to his office, apparently for the express purpose of letting her know he doesn't like her. As he leaves the office the Sunnydale Class of '55 Yearbook falls from his bookshelf, and Buffy picks it up.

Willow is still the substitute teacher for Jenny Calendar and Giles stops at the computer classroom where she tells him about her investigation of Jenny's work. She gives him a rose quartz that belonged to Jenny. In a class Buffy has a waking dream set in 1955. One of the students approaches his female teacher and they surreptitiously hold hands when someone interrupts them. Buffy wakes from the dream to find her teacher writing *"Don't walk away from me, bitch"* on the blackboard. Later Buffy is telling Xander what happened when, as he opens his locker a rotting arm reaches out of it and grabs Xander by the throat. Buffy frees him, and the arm disappears. This is the single false note in an otherwise excellent episode, makes little or no sense in the context of the story and seems to have been filmed purely for shock value. This leads Giles to deduce that paranormal activity is occurring, which may well win him an 'obvious statement of the week' award.

That night Ms Frank, a teacher, passes George the janitor on her way home and they both re-enact the conversation that the young couple held the night before. Giles is working in his office and is disturbed when he hears a female voice call to him. He calls out to Jenny, and walks out to investigate. Giles sees Ms Frank and George just as the gun goes off, the bullet sending Ms Frank over the side of the balcony. Giles tackles George and as the gun is knocked out of his hands we see it vanish. George has no memory of what has happened.

Giles believes the ghost is Jenny. This theory makes little sense to Buffy, Willow, Xander and Cordelia, but Giles remains set in his belief. Willow researches shootings in the school and finds that a student shot his teacher and himself in 1955. Buffy recognises them as the people in her dream and looks them up in the 1955 yearbook. They were James Stanley and his teacher Grace Newman, who were having an affair. Buffy feels James deserved to die after shooting Grace, and it's obvious that much of her vitriol is powered by her feelings for Angelus. In another none-too-logical scene all of the food in the school cafeteria is transformed into snakes, causing a near-riot. Cordelia is bitten by one of the snakes. After the school is evacuated we overhear Principal Snyder talking with a member of the police force, Bob. We learn that Snyder knows that they're on a Hellmouth, and Bob tells Snyder he'd better control the situation otherwise the mayor will have to get involved.

Willow decides independently to exorcise the spirit from the school using Buffy, Xander, and Cordelia to form a Mangus Tripod by chanting from different locations in the school at midnight.

Buffy is in the most dangerous position in the centre of the Tripod. In the school Willow encounters Giles who is trying to contact Jenny Calendar's spirit. As midnight draws near Buffy is drawn to the music room where she sees James dancing with Grace, Cordelia sees the bitten side of her face blister and swell, and an arm comes from the floor near Willow and tries to pull her in. Willow is saved by Giles, and Buffy sees James's face turn into a rotting skull and runs from the music room.

As the group finally performs the chant a swarm of wasps invades the hallways, and they have to evacuate the school. As they leave we can see that swarm surrounds the entire school.

Giles finally comes to the conclusion that it is James' spirit haunting Sunnydale High. He needs to find forgiveness from Grace, but every time he tries, by possessing people and making them re-enact the fatal incident, Grace dies before she can forgive him, so he is doomed to repeat the killing again and again.

While they talk, Buffy is drawn back to the school by a voice only she can hear. The wasps allow her access, and she walks into the school. As she walks the corridors Angelus appears, intending to kill her. As they prepare to fight, James' spirit possesses Buffy and she begins to re-enact out the incident. Angelus, initially thrown off guard by Buffy is possessed by Grace's spirit. In an eerie parallel to Buffy and Angel's doomed love affair they re-enact the fatal incident, with one difference; when Grace is shot, as Angelus is impervious to gunshot her spirit does not disappear. Buffy, possessed by James, makes her way to the music room to shoot herself, but is stopped by Grace in Angelus's body. She forgives him and they share a final kiss before their souls are freed, leaving Buffy and Angelus in a passionate embrace as they leave. When Angelus realises what is happening he pushes Buffy away and bolts.

Buffy finally realises that the shooting was an accident and that what her and James shared was a sense of guilt—he for killing Grace, she for Angelus's murders.

Back at the abandoned garden he shares with Spike and Drusilla, Angelus is still disgusted by being possessed by such a good spirit as Grace. He and Drusilla leave to commit some vile act to wipe away the memory, leaving Spike on his own. When they've gone, the ostensibly crippled Spike rises from his wheelchair and kicks it over.

*The Verdict:* Anyone who's read Alan Garner's *The Owl Service*, a tale of young people possessed by ancient passions, will be powerfully reminded of it by this episode. Some of the effects are bad-horror film tacky, and largely illogical—where, pray, do snakes fit into this story, and why should James shift from poltergeist to possessing spirit? The surprise is that the central story, with its powerful echoing of the Buffy/Angel relationship can more than bear the weight of the tack, and forms one of the best single episodes of the show. The scene where Buffy and Angelus re-enact the incident that leads to Grace's death is painfully poignant, a testament to the work the actors, writers and filmmakers have done in making these characters real for us.

## Go Fish (05/05/98), Episode:5V20

Written by David Fury & Elin Hampton, Directed by David Semel.

At a beach party to celebrate the success of the Sunnydale High swimming team the solitary Buffy is approached by team member Cameron, who seems pleasant and keeps her company. After an incident when Buffy protects Jonathan from another team member, Dodd, Dodd leaves the party with fellow member Gage.

Dodd disappears, with Gage noticing only a strong odour. He doesn't see the serpentine creature leaving what looks like Dodd's remains.

Principal Snyder 'encourages' Willow to give Gage a passing grade in her computer class, as the swimming team's success means a lot to Sunnydale High. Buffy gets into more trouble with Snyder when she breaks Cameron's nose when he turns from pleasant company into amateur rapist on the way to school.

Later Buffy finds out that only Dodd's skin was left, as if he'd been eaten from inside. Xander has an altercation with Cameron, who is going to the cafeteria. As Cameron enters the cafeteria he notices a foul smell. Xander hears a scream and runs to the cafeteria to find all that is left of Cameron is his skin on the floor. As he turns to go he is horrified to be confronted by a gilled and scaly creature with a familial resemblance to the Creature from the Black Lagoon. Xander escapes the creature, and tells Giles about it. Giles realises the killings are connected to the way the swimming team is ranked: Dodd and Cameron were the first and second best swimmers on the team and as Gage is third best, he is probably the creature's next victim. Buffy practises surveillance on Gage, while Willow questions the bullied Jonathan only to learn his idea of revenge is peeing in the school pool. Gage notices the less-than-invisible Buffy and confronts her. Gage doesn't believe her story and leaves, from the frying pan into the fire, as Angelus is his next conversational partner, just prior to sinking his teeth into Gage's neck. Buffy arrives on the scene to see Angelus spitting out Gage's blood. Gage's is discarded by the disgusted vampire who exits stage left still spitting out blood. A chastened Gage asks Buffy to walk him home.

Buffy conjectures that Gage and the team may be taking steroids, which would explain Angelus's repulsion and possibly be the source of their attraction to the creature. Buffy, Willow and Cordelia discover that Xander has joined the team, and looks very good in trunks. Xander is keeping an eye on Gage where Buffy dare not go. Xander and Buffy meet outside the locker room, which Gage is still inside. Gage begins to scream and she enters the locker room to see the creature standing before Gage when to her great surprise Gage peels off his own skin in agony, another creature emerging from the discarded husk. Both of them round on Buffy and one of them bites her arm. Swim team Coach Marin arrives and rescues Buffy as the two creatures escape through a hole in the floor. Marin refutes any idea of steroid abuse in the team.

Xander is deputed to find out about the steroid use from the other team members while Buffy and Willow question Nurse Greenliegh. Unfortunately Coach Marin has his own plans for the portly nurse—as food for the creatures his experiments have created.

Xander discovers he's been exposed to the steroids—they're in the steam of the steam room—and he's not best pleased about it. Under questioning from Buffy, Coach Marin admits to drawing on Russian research about fish DNA to develop his swimming team. He forces Buffy into the same sewer he used to dispose of Nursie, so his boys can satisfy their 'other needs'. In the water, with just the chewed remains of Nursie for company Buffy prepares to fight for her life. Cordelia is near the pool and sees a newly-emerged fish creature, assuming it's Xander—thankfully, it's not, as Xander shows up in time to save her from the creature's attack. In the library Giles has the remaining team members locked safely away.

All roads now point to Coach Marin and after a struggle Xander knocks him into the sewer and extends his arm through the hole for Buffy. She leaps up, grabs Xander's hand, and is pulled to safety, kicking Marin back into the sewer with his team as she does so—with predictably gruesome results. Xander and the rest of the team have to go through a series of blood transfusions that it is hoped will halt the effects of the fist DNA. The last scene shows the fish creatures swimming into the ocean.

*The Verdict:* This is another monster movie remake (this time of *The Creature from the Black Lagoon*) enlivened by strong parts for Xander and Cordelia. The scene where Xander turns up (initially unrecognised) at the swim meet to have his body fulsomely admired by Cordelia, Buffy and Willow, only to shrink off hiding his vital parts when recognised is excellent comedy, as is Cordelia's soliloquy to the fish creature she thinks is Xander.

### Becoming (Part 1) (05/12/98), Episode:5V21

Written & Directed by Joss Whedon.

Angelus's voice-over introduces us to Galway in 1753 and we see a young Angelus drunkenly wandering the streets. His friend collapses and Angelus sees a beautiful blonde woman in a nearby alleyway. As she offers to show him the world beyond Galway we realise that she is Darla. Angelus comes closer to her, she enfolds him in an embrace and sinks her fangs into his neck. Making an incision just above her breasts with her nails she forces Angelus's mouth onto the cut, and Angelus begins his journey into hell.

Sunnydale—the present day. Angelus watches Buffy as she battles a pair of vampires. She orders one of them to tell Angelus that she's taking the offensive, and when he continues to fight finishes him off.

Giles visits Sunnydale Museum, where a large stone artefact has been discovered. Giles interestedly examines the text on the side and asks Doug Perren, the curator, if they have attempted to open it. Giles points out a crack down the side of the stone and asks Doug not to open it until he can decode the text.

London, 1860—Drusilla enters a church and steps into the confessional booth. As she does so an arm falls out from the priest's side of the booth before being pulled back in by Angelus, who has murdered the priest and taken his place. Drusilla confesses to having had visions of the future, and Angelus coolly tells her that she is, indeed, a child of the devil as her family think. Drusilla pleads for help and Angelus allows her to go with instructions to do ten Our Father's and an Act of Contrition.

Sunnydale—present day. Reading about the artefact at the museum in the newspaper, Angelus immediately realises what it is. At Sunnydale High Buffy is being coached in chemistry by Willow when she accidentally drops her pencil. It falls behind the desk right next to Jenny Calendar's disk, which has been there since the night of her murder. Buffy picks up the pencil, missing the disk entirely when she is struck by a strange sense of déjà vu. She repeats dropping the pencil, and this time finds the disk and hands it to Willow, who checks out its contents. They find Jenny Calendar's final project: the curse for the restoration of Angelus's soul. Drusilla, Angelus, and entourage go to the museum to steal the stone, killing Doug Perren in the process.

Rumanian Woods, 1898—An old gypsy woman chants the curse of restoration near the dead body of a gypsy girl stretched out on the ground next to a fire. Glowing beneath the old woman is an Orb of Thesulah, and while she chants Angelus flees through the woods, trying to escape the scene of the crime. As the curse is completed Angelus falls to his knees and his eyes glow as his soul is returned to his body for the first time in over a century. A gypsy elder stands over Angelus, telling him that soon he will remember and have to suffer the guilt for every vile act that he has committed.

Sunnydale—present day. Having been shown a printout of the restoration curse by Buffy and Willow, Giles declares that implementing the curse would need great knowledge of magic. Willow, who has been reading Jenny Calendar's work and monitoring the techno-pagan websites, believes she has sufficient knowledge. Xander is isolated in his belief that Angelus must die for the murders he's committed. He accuses Buffy of being willing to conveniently forget about the Angelus's killings in order to get her boyfriend back.

Angelus tells Spike that the demon Acathla is concealed in the stone artefact that they have stolen from the museum. Acathla can subsume Earth into Hell, but was stopped by a knight centuries ago. His body was turned to stone with the sword still embedded in it and was then placed in the artefact and buried. They open the artefact, revealing the body of Acathla inside. Only someone worthy can remove the sword from Acathla's body, freeing him to rain terror on the world.

At home Buffy finds the claddagh ring that Angel gave to her before he lost his soul. Walking outside she is surprised by Kendra, who has been sent back to Sunnydale to fight a rising dark force that her Watcher has sensed. Kendra shows them a sword that was blessed by the knight who foiled Acathla. If Angelus can revive the demon, the sword may be their last chance. Willow agrees to perform the curse as soon as possible using the Orb of Thesulah that Giles 'happens' to have in his office.

Manhattan, 1996—Angel is stumbling through the streets of Manhattan, dressed like a derelict and living on the blood of rats when he is approached by an allegedly 'good' demon, Whistler, who offers Angel a chance to redeem himself. Whistler says Angel must see something before he can make a decision.

Los Angeles, 1996—Angel observes Buffy's first meeting with a Watcher from a car with painted black windows at Hemery High, her school before Sunnydale High. He follows and sees her learn about her destiny as the Slayer. Angel witnesses her home life and the discord between her parents. Although this contradicts the continuity in the first episode, it is obvious that Angel has fallen in love with Buffy and seeing her causes Angel to ask Whistler to help him.

Sunnydale—present day. Angelus sacrifices a young man, by feeding on his blood, and spreading some on the palm of his right hand. Reciting the incantations for the ritual that will revive Acathla, Angelus approaches his body, grabs the sword and pulls with all his might, but falls to the floor felled by mystical energy. This entertains Spike immensely and upsets Drusilla.

While Buffy and her friends take an exam a female vampire steps into the room, and burns as the rays of the sunlight hit her. She screams out a warning aimed at Buffy that more will die if she doesn't meet Angelus that night. Buffy tells Willow to start the curse and leaves Kendra on guard. She finds and fights Angelus at the cemetery before realising the fight is a diversion to remove her from the library. The library has been invaded by vampires and in the melee Willow is crushed underneath fallen bookshelves, Xander has his arm broken and, as Cordelia escapes from the library, Drusilla enters and kills Kendra, using her hypnotic powers to enthral her, then slashing Kendra's neck with her nails. Kendra falls to the ground with blood pouring from her neck. The vampires leave with the captive Giles just as Buffy makes it to the library. Buffy is discovered by the police leaning over Kendra's fallen body, and is ordered to freeze as one of them holds a gun on her.

## Becoming (Part 2) (05/19/98), Episode:5V22

Written & Directed by Joss Whedon.

The police, believing that Buffy has murdered Kendra, take her outside, as Principal Snyder arrives with more police. Before she can be cuffed, Buffy escapes. Disguising herself (very ineffectively, it must be said) in coat and black woollen hat Buffy goes to the hospital, where she finds the injured Xander, and Willow motionless in a coma. When the somewhat abashed Cordelia arrives Buffy realises that Giles has been kidnapped by Angelus and Drusilla so that Angelus can force him to help them with the ritual to revive Acathla. Investigating Giles' apartment Buffy meets Whistler, who tells her that her relationship has changed Angelus's destiny: he was destined to stop Acathla, not revive him. Buffy leaves, running into a police officer and Spike, who aids her escape. Spike wants Buffy's help to stop Angelus so he can have Drusilla back the way she used to be, and prevent Angelus taking humankind into hell. He explains that he doesn't particularly want to exchange a world of meals on legs for Hell. In return he'll leave town with Drusilla and never return. Buffy takes Spike to her house to put together a plan of attack, but as they arrive both Joyce (newly informed of her daughter's fugitive status) and one of Angelus's crew arrive. Buffy stakes the vampire, rather putting the kibosh on the 'just a normal high school girl' business. Buffy confesses to her remarkably unobservant mother that she is the Slayer.

Willow emerges from her coma just as Xander, who has been trying to talk her back from unconsciousness says he loves her, but her first word is Oz's name, just as he arrives in her room. At Angelus's, Giles refuses to help Angelus, who is torturing him. At Maison Summers Buffy and Spike come to an agreement, but on the conditions that Drusilla leaves with Spike, and Giles survives. When Spike goes, the obtuse Joyce wants an explanation and is somewhat infuriated when Buffy indicates she has more important things on her mind. Joyce isn't greatly enamoured of the 'saving the world' mission (which makes you wonder whether she'd find an eternity in hell plus an obedient daughter a preferable option). Buffy tells her that she didn't want the duty, and an altercation ensues ending in Joyce telling Buffy that if she walks out the door she needn't bother come back. Buffy leaves anyway.

Willow decides to try the curse again. Buffy retrieves the sword that Kendra brought from the library, getting expelled by Principal Snyder on the way. When Buffy goes Snyder makes a phone call to tell the Mayor he has good news. Drusilla uses her hypnotic powers to convince a delirious Giles she is Jenny Calendar and finds out that Angelus's blood is the key to reviving Acathla. Buffy returns to Giles apartment and asks Whistler how to use the sword, and learns that only Angelus's blood can open and close the vortex to Hell. One blow of the sword will close the Vortex, trapping Angelus and Acathla in Hell.

On Buffy's way to the mansion Xander rejoins her and agrees to try and free Giles and escape. He doesn't tell Buffy Willow is trying the curse again.

Inside the mansion, Angelus cuts into his hand, and is about to pull the sword from Acathla's chest when Buffy arrives. Spike rises from his wheelchair and beats Angelus to the floor as Buffy fights the other vampires in the room. Xander frees Giles and escapes with him as Spike is attacked by an enraged Drusilla. Angelus arises, runs to Acathla, grabs the sword with his blooded hand and pulls it out. He turns to find himself in a swordfight with Buffy.

As Willow, Cordelia and Oz perform the curse of restoration Willow becomes possessed by a spirit and performs the curse in Latin. Spike knocks out and Drusilla drags her into a car with painted-black windows and drives from the mansion. As Buffy is about to kill Angelus, Willow completes the curse and Angel's soul is restored. Buffy realises that Angel is back and they embrace, as Acathla awakes, his mouth creating the vortex to Hell. Angel is in complete ignorance of this, so as Buffy kisses him she drives the sword into his stomach releasing the blood that will close the vortex and send Angel and Acathla to Hell. Angel reaches out to Buffy, but all she can do is watch as the vortex closes around Angel, returning Acathla to a statue.

Buffy packs up her troubles in her old kit bag and leaves. When Joyce inspects her room she finds a goodbye letter from her daughter. The last we see of Buffy she is on a bus leaving Sunnydale.

*The Verdict:* At the end of this grueling two-parter the alien on the Mutant Enemy logo (who usually just snarls) says *"I need a hug."* So do the rest of us!

## Season Three

### Regular Cast:

Sarah Michelle Gellar (Buffy Summers), Nicholas Brendon (Xander Harris), Alyson Hannigan (Willow Rosenberg), Charisma Carpenter (Cordelia Chase), David Boreanaz (Angel), Seth Green (Oz), Anthony Stewart Head (Rupert Giles)

### Production Staff Credits

Executive Producer: Joss Whedon , Co-Producer: Marti Noxon, Co-Producer: David Solomon, Producer: Gareth Davies, Executive Producers: Sandy Gallin; Gail Berman; Fran Rubel Kuzui; Kaz Kuzui; David Greenwalt , Executive Story Editor: Jane Espenson, Story Editor: Doug Petrie, Unit Production Manager/Co-Producer: Kelly Manners, First Assistant Director: Brenda Kalosh (all odd-numbered episodes); Steve Hirsch (all even-numbered episodes), Second Assistant Director: Alan Steinman, Score: Christophe Beck, Theme: Nerf Herder, Director of Photography: Michael Gershman, Production Designer: Carey Meyer, Editor: Regis B. Kimble (3ABB01, 3ABB04, 3ABB07); Skip MacDonald (3ABB02, 3ABB05, 3ABB08); Nancy Forner (3ABB03, 3ABB06, 3ABB09), Original Casting: Marcia Shulman, C.S.A., Casting: Brian Meyers, Costume Designer: Cynthia Bergstrom, Production Sound Mixer: David Barr Yaffe, C.A.S., Set Designer: Caroline Quinn, Set Decorator: David Koneff, Leadman: D.C. Gustafson Jr., Construction Coordinator: Stephen L. West, Paint Foreman: Lisa Gamel, Property Master Randy Eriksen, Chief Lighting Technician: Chris Strong, Key Grip: Tom Keefer, Camera Operator: Chris Tufty, Script Supervisor: Rhonda Hyde, Location Manager: Jordana Kronen, Production Auditor: Edwin L. Perez, Stunt Coordinator: Jeff Pruitt, Buffy Stunt Double: Sophia Crawford, Transportation Coordinator: Robert Ellis, Key Hair Stylist: Steve Soussana, Hair Stylist: Lisa Marie Rosenberg, Make-Up Artist: John Maldonado, Special Effects Coordinator: Bruce Minkus, Casting Associate: Jill Uyeda, Production Coordinator: Elyse Ramsdell, Script Coordinator: David Goodman, Assistant to Joss Whedon: Diego Gutierrez, Assistant to David Greenwalt: Robert Price, Production Supervisor: Marc D. Alpert, Post Production Coordinator: Brian Wankum, Assistant Editor: Golda Savage (all odd-numbered episodes); Marilyn Adams (all even-numbered episodes), Post Production Sound: TODD AO STUDIO, Supervising Sound Editor: Cindy Rabideau, Re-Recording Mixers: Kevin Patrick Burns; Todd Keith Orr (3ABB01-3ABB08); Adam Sawelson (3ABB09); Ron Evans, Music Editor: Fernand Bos, Special Make-Up Effects Creator: John Vulich, Make-Up Supervisor: Todd McIntosh, Post Production Services and Visual Effects: Digital Magic, Main Title Design: Montgomery/Cobb, Processing: Deluxe Vampire Design Evolved From Concepts Created by: The Burman Studios.

## Season 3 Episodes

### Anne (09/29/98), Episode:3ABB01

Written & Directed by Joss Whedon.

Buffy is working as a waitress at a small downtown diner, where she goes by the name Anne. Serving a young couple who have just got a distinctive matching tattoo of their names, the girl, Lily, asks if she knows Buffy. Buffy says no and leaves the diner. Lily catches up to Buffy, who she remembers because she was Chantarelle, one of the vampire-wannabe cult in *Lie To Me*. As she thanks Buffy for saving her life an old man pushes his way past them, muttering 'I'm no one,' which seems to be a theme with the derelicts in the area. Buffy runs into Ken, apparently a holy roller, who tells her about Family Home, a centre for runaways.

Lily asks Buffy to find her boyfriend, Rickie, who is missing., and Buffy finally agrees. She finds a dead old man with the distinctive tattoo on his arm. Lily is invited to Family Home by Ken while Buffy breaks into a blood bank the street people sell to and finds Rickie's record marked 'Candidate.' The nurse reluctantly admits that she gives the names of healthy kids to Ken. Buffy pushes her way into Family Home as Lily begins her initiation ritual. Buffy and Ken fight and, with Lily, drop through the cleansing pool into an underground chamber. Ken is revealed to be a demon, and tells them they are trapped in the demon dimension where humans are worked until death. Ken tells them that for every day in Buffy's world a hundred years pass there, and they will be returned to the world above when they are too old.

Buffy regains her identity and proceeds to demolish the overseer and the guards. Lily finds new courage and leads the slaves away, pushing Ken off a ledge as she does so. Buffy kills Ken, and the slaves escape through the portal, which disappears as Buffy and Lily make it through. Lily takes over Buffy's job, name and apartment.

The doorbell rings at the Summers house, and Joyce answers. When she opens it, there stands Buffy, looking sad, tired and dishevelled. For a long moment they just look at each other without saying a word. Then they step toward each other and hold each other close for a long, tight embrace.

## Dead Man's Party (10/06/98), Episode:3ABB02

Written by: Marti Noxon, Directed by: James Whitmore Jr.

Buffy's mother has trouble adjusting to the Slayer thing, but is trying hard. She hangs a Nigerian mask from her gallery on her bedroom wall. When Principal Snyder refuses to let Buffy return to school and Willow fails to meet her, Buffy is bummed out, but returning home she finds Joyce has invited her friends over for dinner the next night. In the basement she finds a dead stray cat, which she and Joyce bury. While they sleep, the eyes of the Nigerian mask glow red and the cat rises and skulks away, growling.

The next morning Joyce opens the back door and the (formerly) dead stray cat runs in. Giles collects kitty, noting the Nigerian mask on Joyce's wall. Buffy's friends decide to turn dinner at Buffy's house into a big party. At the party Buffy asks Willow if they're cool and Willow says they are. The mask's eyes glow and the dead start to rise and shamble towards the Summers house...

Rejected by Xander and Cordelia, and overhearing her mother complain about having her back home, a distraught Buffy goes to her room and starts packing. Willow catches her and starts shouting at her for giving up again. Giles realises that Joyce's mask raises the dead, and speeds off to the Summers house. Joyce walks in on Buffy and Willow's argument, which eventually becomes a free-for-all let's give Buffy a hard time therapy session involving all Buffy's friends. Suddenly (and it's a great relief, believe me) an army of zombies turn up to party, killing guests and letting Buffy do what Buffy does best. Upstairs, one of the undead grabs Pat, a touchy-feely friend of Joyce.

Giles arrives and tells Oz whichever zombie puts on the mask will become a demon incarnate. It's Pat, of course. The demon's power is in its eyes, but Oz is frozen by the demon's eye-flash before he can tell Buffy. Buffy uses the demon's concentration on Oz to put a spade through its face. Pat and the undead disappear immediately.

Giles confronts Snyder about letting Buffy back into school, with a distinct implication of physical violence. Meanwhile Buffy and Willow patch up their relationship.

*The Verdict:* Monster movie frenzy (*Pet Semetary, Night of the Living Dead, The Mask*) ruined by another attempt at social work by Buffy's mom and friends. Let's see; you've saved the world, but had to kill your lover to do it. Just previously your mom told you not to come back if you were foolish enough to go scampering off to save humanity. Nothing that would make you want to run and hide there, right? Presumably Joyce would be happier if Buffy were still in the house, despite the fact said house would now be in hell. With friends like these…

## Faith, Hope & Trick (10/13/98), Episode:3ABB03

Written by David Greenwalt, Directed by James A. Contner.

A limo full of vampires in search of the Slayer pulls into the drive-thru at Sunnydale's Happy Burger. One of the vampires, Mr Trick, picks up a diet soda… and the drive-thru employee himself.

Principal Snyder is forced to readmit Buffy to school if she takes makeup tests and sees a psychologist. At the Bronze Buffy follows a girl and her date as they leave, suspecting the date is a vampire and finds the girl kicking the hell out of her vampiric date. She is a new Slayer named Faith, called by the death of Kendra. She quickly charms Buffy's friends with her outgoing attitude. Even Joyce is taken with Faith and suggests that Buffy could let Faith take over as Slayer.

Mr Trick's cloven-handed master is obsessed by killing the Slayer—Faith. When Buffy and Faith fight a group of vampires Faith sadistically beats one to a pulp without staking him, nearly causing Buffy's death by a vampire who says, *"For Kakistos we live, for Kakistos you die."* Buffy kills both vampires and confronts Faith about her behaviour. Buffy tells Giles and he calls England and finds that Faith's Watcher is dead. Kakistos who is a very old vampire, who Buffy guesses followed Faith to Sunnydale. Buffy confronts Faith about Kakistos and her Watcher and Faith prepares to leave, only to open the door to Kakistos, Trick, and their vampires.

They are herded into the vampire's hideout. Faith says she watched what Kakistos did to her Watcher and ran. Buffy reassures her she did the right thing. Faith freezes before Kakistos; and Buffy intervenes, and seems to be beating Kakistos to the point where the pragmatic Mr Trick ducks out. When Buffy's normal-sized stake isn't enough to finish Kakistos, Faith comes round and shoves a conveniently placed massive wooden pole through the ancient vampire. The Watcher's Council agrees to let Faith stay in Sunnydale until a new Watcher is assigned. Buffy finally tells Willow and Giles that the night she killed Angel Willow's spell worked, and he became Angel again before she kissed him and killed him (which one would conjecture would make them feel pretty poor about their moaning in *Dead Man's Party*.)

That night she places the claddagh ring Angel gave her on the ground where she killed him, and quietly says, 'Goodbye.' A moment later a bright beam of light illuminates the ring on the floor. The ring begins to vibrate and the room is awash with a blindingly bright white light. A body falls through; as the light fades a naked man is lying there. It is Angel.

## Beauty And The Beasts (10/20/98), Episode:3ABB04

Written by: Marti Noxon, Directed by: James Whitmore Jr.

Buffy and Scott Hope, who she has been dating, meet Scott's friends Debbie and Pete. Giles is agitated—there was a death in the woods the previous night with all the marks of a werewolf killing, and it could have been Oz—Xander was sleeping when he should have been watching Oz, and the book cage window is open.

Buffy gives Mr Platt a sanitised version of her relationship with Angel. Platt tells her that you can't stay lost in love forever, or *"love becomes your master… and you're just its dog."* Buffy, patrolling the woods, chases something running through the trees—only to discover it's Angel! They fight, and Buffy knocks him out and chains him up in the mansion. Buffy tells Giles that she dreamed Angel returned. Giles tells her it would take someone of extraordinary will and character to survive the demon dimension and retain any semblance of self. He would have been suffering there for hundreds of years (as we found out in *Anne*).

At the mansion, when she asks Angel if he can understand her he lashes out at her. She returns to Mr Platt's office needing to talk about Angel to discover him dead, horribly mauled. Pete is the killer; he has synthesised a liquid to make him more macho for Debbie, but he now changes into a rage monster. Debbie cradles his head in her arms as he says he's sorry.

It's nearly sundown and Oz is giving Debbie his biology notes, watched by the insanely jealous Pete, when he notices she has a black eye. Oz realises the link between the victims is Debbie and everyone goes to look for Pete and Debbie, while Oz locks himself in the cage. Meanwhile, Angel breaks free of his chains. Buffy and Willow find Debbie, who blames herself for Pete's crime's. Pete attacks Oz, ripping the cage door off. As the sun sets Oz changes into a werewolf, biting Pete, whose scream brings everyone to the library. Oz is subdued by Faith and Willow. Buffy tracks Pete to a storage closet where he has killed Debbie. Their fight is interrupted by the arrival of a fully vampiric Angel who attacks Pete, and kills him. Angel's face reverts to normal.

Angel: *"Buffy?"*

He falls to his knees and holds her tightly and starts to sob. Tears roll down her face.

Scott: *"It's just that you never really know what's going on inside somebody. Do you?"*

Buffy meditates on this as she watches Angel's face contort in pain as he dreams.

## Homecoming (11/03/98), Episode:3ABB05

Written and Directed by David Greenwalt.

While Cordelia and Buffy end up in a competition for Homecoming Queen, sparked by Cordelia's selfishly forgetting to remind Buffy about the yearbook picture-taking session, Mr Trick is recruiting assassins. He has brought a group together including German terrorists, Lyle Gorch (*Bad Eggs*) and his new wife Candy, and a spiny-headed demon named Kulak. Trick says their targets are Buffy and Faith, and welcomes them to 'SlayerFest '98.'

Xander, Willow and Oz are already helping Cordelia's Homecoming Queen campaign, which upsets Buffy, but when she gets into the limo to the dance she finds Cordelia and some corsages in the back instead of Faith. Their friends have set this up to get them talking—but when the limo stops they're stranded in the woods. A videotape of Mr Trick welcomes them to SlayerFest. Buffy and Cordelia are nearly killed by 'Jungle Bob' but persuade him to share his gun and knowledge after trapping him in a bear trap. Kulak the demon is killed by the Germans. At the library Lyle and Candy Gorch have found the weapons stash—Giles lies unconscious.

Buffy and Cordelia enter the library to be attacked by the Gorches. Buffy stakes Candy but is rendered unconscious, as Cordelia fakes out the idiot Lyle by claiming that Buffy is just the runner up—she's the Queen. The Germans arrive and they realise the corsages in the limo conceal tracking devices. Buffy manages to plant a tracking device on one of the Germans and they take each other out. At City Hall the police deliver Mr Trick to the Mayor, who congratulates Trick on SlayerFest, and tells him they're going to get along just fine.

At the Homecoming Dance the Queen is announced. It's a tie—between the other two candidates. Disgusted, Buffy and Cordelia walk out together.

### Band Candy (11/10/98), Episode:3ABB06

Written by Jane Espenson, Directed by Michael Lange.

Buffy and friends are forced to sell chocolate to raise money for new band uniforms. Visiting the depleted Angel, Buffy is busted by Joyce who is waiting for her with Giles who Buffy had claimed to be studying with. After Buffy goes to bed, Joyce and Giles eat some of the chocolate. Meanwhile Ethan Rayne stops a factory worker from eating the chocolate.

Buffy surprises Giles and Joyce, who tell Buffy they're meeting to help divide her time between home and Slaying. Amazingly Joyce lets Buffy use her car. As she leaves, Giles lights up a cigarette and Joyce takes a bottle of booze from hiding. The Bronze is full of adults acting like adolescents and followed by a nerdish Principal Snyder, Buffy and Willow look for Giles, who has gone downtown with Joyce. 'Ripper' knocks out a policeman who tries to stop him and takes his gun. He and Joyce make out on the hood of the policeman's car.

Joyce's car is damaged in an accident with a chocolate intoxicated adult, and Buffy wonders where all the vampires are with the town incapacitated. When someone steals Snyder's chocolate bar he has a fit of the jitters, revealing them to be the source of the trouble. Buffy finds her mother and Giles making out, and with Snyder they head into the factory. They capture Ethan who tells them the chocolate is to render the town helpless while Trick collects a tribute for a demon named Larconis which lives in the sewers. Willow and Oz discover Larconis is a demon requiring a ritual feeding of babies every thirty years: the tribute is newborn babies, from the maternity ward of the hospital.

Buffy fights Trick's vampires in the sewers while Giles and Joyce take the babies to safety. A vampire thrown into the sewer is promptly eaten by Larconis, so Trick throws Giles in, while he escapes. Buffy rescues Giles by using a gas main to set Larconis on fire. Trick tells the Mayor he did him a favour by removing a demon he had to pay tribute to. The mayor warns Trick about doing him too many more favours.

### Revelations (11/17/98), Episode:3ABB07

Directed by James A. Contner, Written by Douglas Petrie.

Faith's new Watcher, Gwendoline Post, arrives, telling them that a demon named Lagos is coming to Sunnydale in search the Glove of Myhnegon, which is hidden in one of Sunnydale's twelve cemeteries. Angel seems to recognise the name of Lagos. Giles finds that the Glove is hidden in the von Hauptmann family crypt and Xander offers to go to tell Buffy. Xander sees Angel emerging from the crypt with the Glove and, tailing him back to the mansion, sees him kiss Buffy.

When Buffy arrives with the news about the glove Giles tells her they know that Angel is alive. Buffy insists that Angel is better. Both Xander and Giles are unimpressed, Giles reminding her that Angel tortured him:

Giles: *"You have no respect for me, or the job I perform."*

Giles tells Mrs Post about Angel having the Glove, and that the Glove can be destroyed by being using living flame. For his reward Mrs Post clubs him into unconsciousness.

At the von Hauptmann crypt, Buffy fights and beheads Lagos but returns to find Giles on a stretcher. Mrs Post finds Angel doing the living flame ritual himself, cons the Glove out of him then drops him with a shovel. He gets right back up in vampire mode and attacks her. Faith arrives, assumes the obvious, and is about to stake Angel when Buffy arrives and tries to talk her out of it, but the two Slayers fight their way through the windows into the courtyard. Willow and Xander arrive with the living flame catalyst. Willow helps Mrs Post get the Glove of Myhnegon, and another falls as Mrs Post puts on the Glove. Faith asks Gwendolyn what's going on:

Gwendolyn: *"Faith! A word of advice: you're an idiot!"*

Mrs Post hurls lightning from the Glove at the two Slayers. As Mrs Post tries to kill Faith, Buffy severs Mrs Post's Glove-wearing arm with glass from the courtyard windows, and Mrs Post is consumed by lighting. Having disposed of the Glove everyone is still unsure about Angel. Buffy goes to Faith's apartment and tries to convince Faith that she's on Faith's side. Faith doesn't seem convinced.

As Buffy leaves, Faith says, *"I'm on my side. That's enough."*

## Lovers Walk (11/24/98), Episode:3ABB08

Directed by David Semel, Written by Dan Vebber.

As Buffy takes in the news she's qualified for University a car runs over the Welcome to Sunnydale sign, and a drunk Spike emerges, heading for the burnt remnants of the warehouse. Drusilla has left him. Buffy talks to Giles about the possibility of going to a college outside Sunnydale while Faith becomes the local Slayer. Mayor Wilkins discovers that Spike is back in town and gets Mr Trick to send a welcoming committee. Spike goes to a local magic shop to find a curse for Angel, and sees Willow leaving with the ingredients for a charm to stop her wanting Xander. After she leaves, Spike feeds on the shopkeeper and makes a new plan to get what he wants. Spike kidnaps Willow, knocking Xander out. At the warehouse Xander is laid out, unconscious and bloody, as Spike demands Willow perform a love spell that will bring Drusilla back to him. Willow tells Spike she still needs additional ingredients and the right spell book. Buffy answers a phone call from Joyce and is horrified to hear Spike's voice in the background—she runs home as fast as she can.

Joyce makes coffee while Spike unburdens himself about Drusilla. Angel is outside Buffy's house and sees Spike sitting with Joyce; he tries to run into the house, but can't do so without an invitation. Joyce is terrified by Angel, unaware that Spike is the real enemy. Spike tells Buffy and Angel what he's done with Willow and Xander, but won't say where they are until they agree to help him get what he needs for the love spell.

Oz picks up Willow's scent and tries to find Willow and Xander instead. Buffy and Angel go to the magic shop to get the ingredients. Spike mocks Buffy and Angel's attempts to be just friends, telling them that they will be in love with each forever, just like he is with Drusilla. Xander finally comes to and learns from Willow everything that's happened. With their situation is seemingly hopeless, Xander and Willow lay on the bed and kiss, unaware that Oz and Cordelia have just arrived to rescue them. Cordelia takes it hard and falls through one of the deteriorated steps as she runs away, impaling herself on a steel rod.

Spike, Buffy, and Angel finally run into Mr Trick's vampires and battle commences. They retreat but battle spills into the magic shop. The vampires are driven off by vials of holy water thrown by Buffy and Angel. Spike decides to win Drusilla back by returning to his old self, and tells them where Willow and Xander are and leaves. Xander climbs down to Cordelia while Oz goes to get help. The next day, Willow tells Buffy that she used to want everything, now she just wants Oz to talk to her again. Xander brings Cordelia flowers in the hospital, but she tells him to stay away from her, and Buffy tells Angel she won't be going to see him anymore, because Spike was right. *"What I want from you I can never have,"* she tells him. Everyone is quite unhappy... except Spike, who speeds off to win his woman back, singing along to Gary Oldman's version of Sid Vicious's version of *My Way* (if you see what I mean...)

### The Wish (12/08/98), Episode:3ABB09

Written by: Marti Noxon, Directed by: David Greenwalt.

Cordelia, desperately hurt by Xander's betrayal finds that only Anya, a new girl, offers support and friendship. When a slaying ends up with Cordelia covered in trash, just in time for her ex-friends to mock her, Cordelia complains to Anya that Buffy's arrival in Sunnydale was the source of all her problems. Anya gives Cordelia her necklace as a gift and Cordelia wishes Buffy Summers had never come to Sunnydale.

Anya: *"Done!"*

In a flash Anya and half the students in the courtyard are gone. Cordelia is in a reality where Buffy didn't come to Sunnydale and is popular again. When Cordelia asks if Xander and Willow are miserable, Harmony tells her they're dead. Sunnydale has turned into a ghost town. Cordelia runs into vampire versions of Willow and Xander and, after she mentions Buffy, is only saved from them by the arrival of Giles wielding a large cross. Willow and Xander go to the Bronze, now the home of the Master, who they tell about Cordelia and her mention of Buffy. The Master is annoyed at the possibility of a Slayer coming to Sunnydale because 'the plant' is set to open the next night. He sends them after Cordelia, who is trying to explain about Anya to Giles. Xander and Willow lock Giles in the book cage and as he watches they drink Cordelia's blood, killing her.

Oz and Larry return and as they take Cordelia's body away Giles notices Anya's necklace around her neck and takes it. Willow and Xander report Cordelia's death to the Master, who lets Willow 'play with the puppy'—a caged and chained Angel, who she tortures while Xander watches. Giles phones Buffy's Watcher and ask for her, and then finds the necklace is the symbol of Anyanka, a patron saint of scorned women who grants wishes. On the way home, as he rescues a group of people from some vampires, someone else joins the fight. Looking up he see a scarred, unhappy-looking Buffy Summers, who demands to know why she's been called.

Giles finds out that Anyanka can be defeated by destroying her 'power centre' but Buffy sets out to slay the Master. She finds the Bronze empty and frees Angel and together they head to the plant, where the Master makes a grand speech about the wonders of mass production—the automated extraction of blood from humans. As Buffy and Angel attack the Master, Giles summons Anyanka, who threatens him. He pulls off her necklace as Buffy and the Master get ready for final battle. Giles smashes the necklace as the Master breaks Buffy's neck. Everything returns to normal, except that Anya is mortal and powerless, and has to listen to Cordelia's list of wishes, but is unable to grant any of them.

*The Verdict:* A Buffy-style remake of *It's a Wonderful Life*, that gives the cast a chance to flex their acting muscles and draws a frightening picture of Sunnydale *sans* Buffy.

## Amends (12/15/98), Episode:3ABB10

Written and Directed by Joss Whedon.

Angel runs into Buffy doing her Christmas shopping. In the crowd he sees Daniel, a man he killed 180 years ago. He becomes tormented with dreams of his past killings and goes to Giles for help. Angel wants to know why he isn't still in a demon dimension enduring an eternity of suffering—who released him and why, but is distracted by the apparition of Jenny Calendar. Giles can't see her, so is baffled when Angel runs out of the door. At the mansion Angel dreams about killing a servant named Margaret and, in the dream, looks up to see Buffy watching. Angel awakes... as does Buffy. Shopping for a tree Buffy sees an area of completely dead trees. Joyce tells Buffy to invite Faith over for Christmas, which she does to little response.

In the mansion Angel's dreams have intruded into his waking life and the shades of Jenny, Daniel, Margaret, and other victims haunt him. Buffy explains to Giles that she shared Angel's dream the previous night—including things she couldn't know about him. She's put Angel behind her, but she can't break free while she is trapped into his dreams. Giles, Buffy, Xander and Willow decide to help Angel and research what is happening. Buffy and Angel fall asleep and share a dream; they are making love in Buffy's bedroom, when Buffy sees an eyeless priest over Angel's shoulder. Angel transforms into his vampire self and bite into Buffy's neck, waking them both up. Jenny Calendar tells Angel that only losing his soul with Buffy again and killing her will bring him peace. Giles finds out about the eyeless men—the Bringers, or Harbingers. These high priests can summon The First, the name given to Absolute Evil, and that would have had the power to bring Angel back. Buffy and Xander go to Willy's bar and learn that the Bringers might be underground. It's Christmas Eve and they go home, planning to resume their search.

Faith appears bearing gifts for Buffy and Joyce. Buffy, fetching gifts, finds Angel in her bedroom. The shade of Jenny Calendar is urging him to take her, but Angel throws himself through Buffy's window. Angel decides to kill himself with the sun. Leaving Faith to guard her mother's safety, Buffy goes to Giles' to find out where the Bringers are. No life can grow above or below the Bringers, and Buffy remembers the dead trees. Buffy breaks open the ground, finds the Bringers and takes them out. Jenny Calendar appears to her, speaking for The Firs, telling her Angel will die by sunrise. She finally finds Angel on a hill which overlooks Sunnydale. Angel tells her that he can't go on living, knowing his existence threatens Buffy's life. Buffy refuses to agree, telling Angel that it's harder to live, but it's what they have to do. Snow begins falling from the sky preventing the sun's rays from ending Angel's life. Angel has yet another lease on life... at Christmas.

### Gingerbread (01/12/99), Episode:3ABB11

Directed by James Whitmore Jr., Written by Thania St. John & Jane Esperson, Teleplay by Jane Esperson.

Observing Buffy's slaying exploits in the cause of 'sharing' Joyce Summers discovers a dead boy and girl, at a nearby playground; a symbol is drawn in black in the palms of their hands. Giles thinks the symbol indicates the work of a cult. Joyce organises a meeting at City Hall to discuss the murder, which dozens of parents attend, including Sheila, Willow's uncommunicative mom. Joyce calls for the grown-ups to take action against the supernatural.

Giles asks Buffy to get a book from Willow for him. Doing this, Buffy notices the symbol from the children's hands is drawn on Willow's notebook. Willow tells Buffy that the symbol is for a protection spell that she wanted to cast for Buffy's upcoming birthday—it's completely harmless. The police search the school for evidence of witchcraft and Amy, Willow and Giles go off with them. Joyce founds MOO (Mothers Opposed to the Occult); the two dead children appear to her, and she listens to them intently as they beg her to make their murderers suffer. Sheila grounds Willow for getting into trouble at school.

Meeting Giles, Xander, and Oz, Buffy points out that nobody seems to know the children's names or where they came from. Oz emails Willow, who finds out on the Web that the dead bodies of these same two children have been repeatedly discovered once every fifty years. The oldest article identifies them as Hans and Greta Strauss—Hansel and Gretel must have been based on them. Amy is taken from her home, and Willow answers the knocking at her door to find her mother and a group of angry parents who want her death. Buffy and Giles interrupt a MOO meeting and Giles is knocked unconscious while Joyce chloroforms Buffy.

Buffy, Willow, and Amy are tied to stakes in City Hall, ready to be burned for Witchcraft. Buffy finally regains consciousness, but Joyce refuses to listen to her daughter's pleas. Amy transforms herself into a rat and bolts from the room, leaving Willow and Buffy moments away from a fiery death. Giles and Cordelia arrive and while Cordelia extinguishes the fire, Giles casts a spell on the two children, who combine and become a tall, hideous demon, which attempts to kill Buffy and Willow. Buffy breaks the stake she's been tied to in half and impales the demon on it.

Later, Buffy and Willow talk about Sheila Rosenberg's selective memory concerning the demon, just like the way Joyce Summers' memory used to operate before learning that her daughter was the Slayer. Willow tries to restore the Amy rat to human form, but fails, and Buffy suggests that perhaps they should get her a *"one of those wheel thingies."*

## Helpless (01/19/99), Episode:3ABB12

Directed by James A. Contner, Written by David Fury.

Buffy's Slayer powers seem to be fading but Giles assures Buffy that she'll be okay. With her birthday approaching she is upset to find her father can't take her to the traditional ice show. At the deserted Sunnydale Arms boarding house we see three men. Two of them cover the windows with bricks, as the third, an older English gentleman, says that *"the Slayer's preparation is nearly complete"*. They have an insane vampire inside a human-sized, padlocked crate, who must be fed pills at regular intervals. Buffy hints to Giles that he might like take her to the ice show, but he makes her study the fault inside a large blue stone. Buffy falls into a trance, and then he injects a strange, green fluid into Buffy's arm.

Buffy's powers continue to wane. Giles speaks with the older man, Quentin, at the boarding house, disagreeing with the Watcher Council's insistence on subjecting Buffy to the Cruciamentum—a test which all Slayers must endure when they reach the age of eighteen in order to prove their instinctual skills and resourcefulness. Buffy must defeat an insane vampire, Zackary Kralik, in the confines of this boarding house. While Buffy search for a reason for her loss of power, Kralik escapes from his box... soon one of the Watchers is also a vampire.

Giles finds Kralik's tomb empty and runs to find Buffy. She has been found by Kralik and runs for her life. Giles rescues her and tells the whole truth to Buffy, showing her the syringe filled with muscle relaxants and adrenal suppressers. Furious Buffy goes home, only to find a Polaroid of her mother and Kralik. She packs a large amount of her slaying supplies into her bag and heads towards the boarding house.

Buffy walks in through the main entrance of the boarding house and the vampire Watcher, Blair, locks the main entrance, trapping the Slayer inside. Quentin visits Giles and tells him that the Cruciamentum has begun. Giles leaves Quentin in the library and races towards the boarding house. Buffy encounters Kralik and tries to take him out with her crossbow, but it's no use. Kralik finally traps her in the hallway and Buffy tries to ward him off with a cross, but Kralik is so insane that he actually enjoys the pain. Kralik is hit by a need for his pills, but Buffy grabs them and dives through a laundry chute, finding Joyce in the basement. When Kralik reaches the basement, he rips the bottle out of her hands and grabs the nearby glass of water. Kralik notices a burning sensation inside himself. Buffy holds out an empty bottle of Holy Water, and Kralik disintegrates. Giles and Blair crash into the basement, and Giles kills the vampire, then leaves with Joyce and Buffy.

Quentin commends Buffy on her successful passing of the test, but Giles is relieved of his duties as Buffy's Watcher because he has a father's love for her. He tells Buffy she will be assigned a new Watcher soon, as Giles tends to her wounds.

## The Zeppo (01/26/99), Episode:3ABB13

Directed by James Whitmore Jr, Written by Dan Vebber.

Xander, aware of his lack of a special skill or powers compared to the rest of the team is deemed to be 'The Zeppo'—the useless one—(a cruel reference to the fifth Marx Brother) by Cordelia. Giles has bad news—an Apocalypse cult called the

Sisterhood of Jhe intends to reopen the Hellmouth, soon.

The only thing that Xander can come up with to help him fit in is a car, which gets him a date with Lysette, a beautiful but dull girl, but little else. The Watcher Council are unwilling to listen to Giles, so he tries to contact spirit guides for help. Buffy goes to Willy's bar to find a beaten Willy warning her that the Hellmouth will be opened before sunrise.

Xander crashes his car into local psychopath Jack O'Toole's and just before Jack knifes him, a cop shows up. Xander covers for Jack and impressed, Jack invites Xander to hang out with him. Xander drives Jack and Lysette to the cemetery where they're supposed to meet up with Jack's friends. Jack's are somewhat... dead. Lysette screams and runs as Jack uses a ritual to raise one of his friends, Bob, from the grave. Xander takes this in his stride—the dead seem more interested in partying and whether Jack has taped *Walker Texas Ranger* for them than anything else. While Jack raises two more guys, Xander sees Giles and offers his help, but Giles advises him to stay out of it. Xander's friends have him drive them to the hardware store. While they break in and loot the place, Xander sees Willow and again, he asks if she needs any help but she turns him down. Jack and his friends decide to initiate Xander into their group, the sole requirement for which is death. Xander argues that Jack isn't dead, only to have Jack reveal the bullet holes in his abdomen. Xander makes a run for it, getting back in his car and speeds away. He sees Faith battling a Sisterhood of Jhe member and rams his car into the demon, taking off with Faith. In her motel room Faith is all worked up and wants sex, kicking him out as soon as they finish.

The bags in the back seat of his car contain the ingredients for a bomb; Xander would like to know what they'd be likely to blow up. Buffy, at the mansion with Angel, is too busy arguing so Xander returns to school. Finding the zombie boys he grabs one of them and hits the gas. The bomb is in the boiler room of Sunnydale High but the zombie is decapitated before he gets the info he needs to disarm the bomb. Xander runs inside the school, unaware that the rest of his friends are in a life-and-death battle with the Hellmouth demon in the library... again. Xander takes out the zombies one by one. In the boiler room

Xander dares a knife-wielding Jack to let the bomb explode and permanently end his days as one of the walking dead. Jack disarms the bomb and after Xander leaves the boiler room has a fatal encounter with werewolf Oz.

The next morning Oz tries to figure out why he's so full. Cordelia tries to make fun of Xander, but he now has quiet confidence in his abilities.

*The Verdict:* Like a demented voodoo version of *After Hours* this is one of the most entertaining episodes of season three. Nicholas Breedon gets to show off all his comedic/dramatic acting chops in what is virtually a showreel for his abilities.

## Bad Girls (02/09/99), Episode:3ABB14

Directed by Michael Lange, Written by Douglas Petrie.

Buffy and Faith fights a vampire wielding a pair of swords, but when they kill him the two swords have disappeared. Mr Trick has taken them to the Mayor, who reminds Mr Trick and his deputy mayor of the upcoming dedication and the hundred days which will ultimately lead to the ascension.

Buffy meets her new Watcher, Wesley Wyndam-Pryce, who identifies the vampire packing the two swords as a member of a fifteenth-century duellist cult called El Eliminati. They once worked for Balthazar, an ancient demon, before he was killed. Wesley thinks they may be looking for an amulet hidden in the Gleaves family crypt. Faith arrives, meets Wesley, and immediately leaves, telling Buffy that they don't have to follow their new Watcher's orders. As Buffy locates the amulet Eliminati vampires enter the crypt and take it. Faith arrives and they go after the vampires, recovering the amulet.

Wesley inspects the amulet while Buffy skips class to follow Faith to a vampire nest, which they destroy. With a buzz on, Buffy and Faith head to the Bronze and party. Angel warns Buffy that Balthazar is still alive. Buffy takes the amulet from Wesley and gives it to Angel for safekeeping. Buffy and Faith spy Balthazar's gathering in a warehouse and break into a hunting equipment shop for weapons, a spree that degenerates into wanton destruction. Arrested, they cause the car to crash and escape.

Mayor Wilkins is attacked by Vincent, one of the Eliminati,

in his own office Wilkins orders Mr Trick to lock him up. As Wesley and Giles argue over the former Watcher's performance with Buffy, Giles notices the sudden presence of several vampires outside the office. Buffy and Faith head to the warehouse to take out Balthazar and co. On the way they fight with vampires and dust them, but when a hand grabs Buffy, Faith stakes Deputy Mayor Allan Finch. Faith and Buffy split up, Buffy running into Angel, who notices the blood on her hands. At the warehouse Giles and Wesley have been brought before Balthazar. Wesley attempts to save himself by offering the man who has the amulet to Balthazar. When Angel and Buffy arrive Balthazar uses his telekinesis to bring Angel into his own hands, but Buffy electrocutes the obese demon. With his last breath, Balthazar warns Buffy that a greater enemy's ascension is at hand. Mayor Wilkins performs the dedication ritual in his office and frees Vincent from his cage. Vincent cleaves the mayor's head into two halves, then watches in horror as it reforms itself. Mayor Wilkins is now invincible, and he will remain so for the hundred days leading to his ascension.

Buffy visits Faith's motel room the next morning to discuss the murder. Faith shows no guilt and tells Buffy she returned to the scene of the crime and dumped the body.

### Consequences (02/16/99), Episode:3ABB15

Directed by Michael Gershman, Written by Marti Noxon.

Buffy is tormented by nightmares of Finch's death, but is ironically assigned with Faith to investigate it. Mayor Wilkins is shredding Finch's files and wondering if Allan Finch was conspiring against him somehow. Buffy and Faith check out Finch's office to try and explain why he was in the alley that night. Finding nothing Buffy believes that a cover-up is going on. They see Mayor Wilkins and Mr Trick enter the building together. Buffy still can't believe that Faith is okay with murdering a man, but Faith believes that being Slayers should put them above the law.

Buffy tells Willow the truth about everything that happened and she advises Buffy to go to Giles. Faith has got there first and has blamed Buffy for the killing. Giles assures Buffy that he's aware of Faith's lies. Wesley overhears this and he calls Watcher's Council in Britain to tell them of the crime.

Xander volunteers to talk to Faith, immediately alerting Buffy, Willow, and Giles to the fact he's slept with Faith. Xander tries to help Faith see that what she did was wrong, but she tries kill him, only stopped by a bat wielding Angel. Faith regains consciousness in the mansion and tries to come on to Angel. Angel tells Buffy he thinks Faith has a taste for killing now. When she leaves he tries to talk to Faith, but the mansion is invaded by Wesley and a team of men who subdue Angel while Wesley takes the Slayer in a truck to face the Council. Faith easily escapes the witless Wesley.

Buffy tracks Faith to the docks where she is ready to flee the country, where they're both ambushed by Mr Trick and his vampire cohorts. Faith saves Buffy from certain death staking Mr Trick from behind. Buffy talks to Giles about Faith's heroic act, believing there may still be hope for Faith. Unfortunately, aware Mr Trick has vacated his position, Faith has applied to Mayor Wilkins for the job.

## Doppelgängland (02/23/99), Episode:3ABB16

Written & Directed by Joss Whedon.

Anyanka wants to find someone who will help her retrieve her power centre from the alternative reality Cordelia visited in *The Wish,* and asks the currently much put-upon Willow, who is tired of being the goody-two-shoes of the group. Anyanka introduces herself as Anya, a friend of Cordelia's, and persuades Willow to perform a spell to create a temporal fold. Anya says she wants to retrieve a lost necklace which was a family heirloom. When they perform the spell, Willow sees the alternate universe that Cordelia visited, but instead of retrieving the necklace the vampire Willow is transported out just moments before she was killed.

After night falls, Willow from the alternate reality ventures out onto the streets of Sunnydale, and heads to the Bronze, where she draws stares from everybody in attendance. She pulls Xander into her arms and realises that Xander is still human. Buffy arrives tries to stop her leaving, but Willow spins around in vampire guise. She takes off leaving a horrified Xander and

Buffy. Encountering Alfonse and another of Mayor Wilkins' vampires she convinces them to work for her and restore chaos to Sunnydale.

Lamenting Willow's death Buffy and co. are overjoyed and somewhat confused when the Willow of their reality enters the library. Angel goes to the Bronze in search of Buffy in time to meet the alternative Willow and her newly hired cohorts. Anya explains everything to the lost vampire, telling her that this reality's Willow can send her back to where she belongs. Staying to get a tranquiliser gun, while the others go to the Bronze, Willow encounters her mirror image. Willow tranquillises her and when Buffy and co. return they lock the alternative Willow inside the book cage.

Willow disguises herself as the vampire Willow and enters the Bronze. Vampire Willow wakes up in the bookcage dressed in Willow's clothes, and tricks Cordelia into releasing her. Wesley rescues Cordelia and vampire Willow leaves. At the Bronze Willow's charade is detected and the others enter the Bronze and battle the remaining vampires.

Willow stops Buffy from killing her alternative self and prepares another temporal fold. The vampire Willow is returned to the alternate reality just in time to be killed by Oz.

## Enemies (03/16/99), Episode:3ABB17

Written by Douglas Petri, Directed by David Grossman.

On patrol with the newly cleared Faith, Buffy is approached by a demon who wants $5,000 for the Books of Ascension, which he intimates are of particular interest to Mayor Wilkins. Faith tells the Mayor, who instructs her to kill the demon and retrieve the books.

Giles finds that on a previous Ascension, an entire town was apparently wiped out. Faith tracks the demon and kills him. Faith stares at his blood on her hands for a moment, visibly shaken. Later that night, Faith visits Angel at the mansion and shows him her hands which are still stained with the demon's blood. Angel embraces her for comfort and Faith tries to initiate a kiss, but Angel backs off. Unnoticed, Buffy witnesses Faith giving him a small kiss on the cheek as she leaves. Faith tells Mayor Wilkins that she failed in her plan to give Angel the moment of true happiness required to remove his soul.

Buffy and Faith 'find' the dead demon at Wesley's instruction and Buffy realises there's something wrong with Faith's behaviour. Mayor Wilkins has engaged a shrouded man to remove a soul. Buffy tells Willow about Angel and Faith and Willow assures Buffy that she has nothing to worry about. Faith is at the mansion and douses a dark liquid onto Angel's chest. The shrouded man surrounds Angel in a field of energy and he falls to the floor, Angelus again. Faith whips out her stake and forces Angelus to listen to her. Faith leads him to the Mayor's office. At the Mayor's office Angelus tries to kill Mayor Wilkins and learns of his invulnerability. Angelus and Faith are ordered to take care of the other Slayer in town. They beat Xander up on the way to Buffy's house, where they use the Books of Ascension to lure Buffy to the mansion.

At the Hall of Records an old photograph of Mayor Wilkins reveals he must be over a hundred years old. Xander tells them about the return of Angelus. Buffy follows Angelus and Faith to the mansion, where they knock her out and tie her up in chains. Faith tells Buffy she couldn't stand being in Buffy's shadow ever since she arrived in Sunnydale. Buffy tells Faith she can stop the Mayor's Ascension. Faith tells them the Ascension cannot be stopped and will take place on Graduation Day. Angel drops the Angelus act, and Buffy escapes from the chains supposedly restraining her. Faith realises that it was a set-up and attacks Buffy. The others arrive in time to see Angel falling towards them. As Angel and Xander go down, Faith escapes from the mansion.

With the information concerning the Ascension and its date to discuss, Buffy reminds Xander Angel was only acting when he punched him, but disturbed by memories of what Angel could become again, Buffy puts their relationship on hold.

### Earshot (09/21/99), Episode:3ABB18

Written by Jane Espenson, Directed by Regis Kimble.

*The mass murder of 13 students at Littleton, Colorado, on April 20, 1999, by two boy who later killed themselves prompted WB not to air this episode. The second part of the third season finale,* Graduation Day, Part Two, *was also affected although it had already aired in parts of Canada.* Graduation Day, Part Two *was aired on July 13th 1999.*

Killing a demon on patrol, Buffy's hand comes in to contact with its blood. Giles reveals she may be infected with an aspect of the demon, which cheers her up not at all. The next day she finds that she can hear the thoughts of others. In class, she hears the thoughts of Freddy Iverson who has a negative opinion about everything at Sunnydale.

She tries to read Angel's mind to find out what happened with Faith, but can't because he's a vampire. He tells her that in 243 years, he's loved only Buffy. At school she is assaulted by the thoughts of her friends and classmates and in the lunchroom hears someone think, *"By this time tomorrow, I'll kill you all,"* and then passes out. Organising everyone to find out who the potential killer is, Buffy overhears Giles thinking that her power may drive her insane. Buffy's mom is nervous and Buffy finds out that she had sex with Giles, twice, on the hood of a police car.

Giles and Wesley find a solution to curing Buffy, but it requires the heart of the second demon. Angel hunts down the demon and brings the heart to the Summers home in a potion and forces Buffy to drink it. When she wakes up she is no longer able to hear thoughts. They think they've found the killer when they find a letter from Jonathan apologising for his upcoming actions of death on Freddy's desk. Buffy goes to the clocktower and takes a rifle from him. But Jonathan was going to commit suicide, not murder...

Xander stumbles on the lunchroom cook putting rat poison into the food, and Buffy saves him from a filleting by knocking her unconscious. It bugged her that the students could eat so much junk food and not gain much weight. Giles asks her if she's up for training, and Buffy says she is if he isn't too busy sleeping with her mother.

Giles walks straight into a tree.

### Choices (05/04/99), Episode:3ABB19

Written by Jane Espenson, Directed by Regis Kimble.

Faith runs an errand for Mayor Wilkins to the airport. The courier expects payment, but a clearly out of control Faith just kills him and takes the box he's carrying, cutting off his hand with a dagger that Mayor Wilkins has given her as a present to retrieve it.

Buffy is worried about which college she should go to, finally deciding to leave Sunnydale. Wesley tells her she can't leave with Faith gone bad and the Mayor's ascension coming up. Wesley says they could consider it if Buffy stops the Mayor's ascension, so she decides to take the fight to the enemy. At City Hall she sees Faith bringing the box to the Mayor. Buffy interrogates the driver of the limo that dropped Faith off and finds that the box is the Box of Gavroc, housing demonic energy that the Mayor must devour before Ascension Day. They concoct a potion to break the shield that protects the Box of Gavroc. Buffy, Willow and Angel climb to the top of City Hall, dissolve the protective shield and lower Buffy through the skylight and down to the box. As she removes the box the alarms go and the harness gets stuck. Angel drops down into the room and they fight off Mayor Wilkins' vampires and escape from City Hall. They don't realise that Faith has captured Willow.

Buffy decides to trade the box back to the Mayor in exchange for Willow over Wesley's protests. Willow escapes from her shackles and wanders City Hall, eventually finding the Books of the Ascension which she reads. Faith finds her and is going to kill her when Mayor Wilkins enters with details of the trade. The trade is to be made in the school cafeteria but before it's completed, Principal Snyder enters with two policemen in tow. In the chaos that ensues Faith and the Mayor escape with the Box of Gavroc, but leave behind Faith's dagger. Willow has torn a selection of pages from the Books of Ascension.

Willow has decided to stay at home and go to UC-Sunnydale so she can stay with Buffy. They'll be able to stay together as friends. Willow has realised she wants to fight evil, and help people, and she feels she can do that best in Sunnydale.

## The Prom (05/11/99), Episode:3ABB20

Written by Marti Noxon Directed by David Solomon.

It's time for the Prom and Anya, still a mere human being, asks Xander to the Prom and he says yes. Joyce tells Angel that he's affecting Buffy's future and he must leave her alone. Meanwhile, in a small house, someone plays a video for a caged demon. Angel tells Buffy he plans to leave Sunnydale if they survive the Ascension. Willow comforts Buffy, but Buffy realises that Angel was right; the two of them can't be together and she cries. The caged demon escapes. At *April Fools,* a dress shop, Xander spots Cordelia through the window and goes in to talk. She's working there because her family lost all of their money and have nothing and she can't afford to go to college. The beast that broke free breaks through the window and kills a boy dressed in a tux.

Watching the attack on the security tape they spot Tucker Wells, one of Oz's classmates. Tucker intends to ruin prom night by sending a hellhound trained to attack students in formal wear. Buffy isn't going to let the prom be spoiled and everyone splits up to look for clues. Leaving work, Cordelia finds that Xander has paid for her prom dress.

Buffy has found Tucker and tells everyone to go to the prom while she deals with him. She ties Tucker up in his basement but finds out that there are dogs already on their way to the school. She intercepts and kills the dogs, then changes into her prom dress and shows up for the party. Everyone just enjoys the evening.

At Class awards Buffy is awarded Class Protector. Thanks to her the Sunnydale class of '99 has the lowest mortality rate of any class at Sunnydale and they are aware that it's down to Buffy. Finally Angel shows up in a tux and they slowly dance together.

*The Verdict:* With Buffy knowing heartbreak for her and Angel is approaching, this is a heartwarming episode, with the tribute to her from the students genuinely moving.

## Graduation Day, Part One (05/18/99), Episode:3ABB21

Written & Directed by Joss Whedon.

Graduation day is here and Mayor Wilkins is guest speaker. Faith is preparing his way by killing Professor Worth. Xander mentions the Ascension to Anya and it turns out that not only does she know what it is, she's been to one. In 1800 in the Urals a sorcerer achieved Ascension and became the embodiment of the demon Lohesh. Lohesh, a four-winged soul killer, decimated the village within hours—only three people survived. Anya explains all the demons that walk the earth are tainted or hybrids—an Ascension means that a human being becomes pure demon. She doesn't think this is Lohesh, though, because the rituals are different. As she says this, the Mayor bursts into the library, and boast of the fact he'll eat Buffy when the Ascension comes. Giles stabs the Mayor with his fencing foil but the invulnerable city official walks away, chuckling about his commencement address.

Buffy investigates Professor Worth's apartment with Angel. Outside the professor's apartment, Faith shoots Angel through the back with a poisoned arrow and Buffy rushes him to the library. Giles and Wesley discus why the professor's research was of interest to the Mayor. He had found a large carcass buried by a volcanic eruption and Giles thinks that it could be a demon—which would imply that demons can be killed. The mayor is only impervious to harm until the Ascension—once in demon form, he can be killed.

Buffy resigns as a Slayer when the Council decline to help Angel. The only cure for the poison is the blood of a slayer. Buffy decides to use Faith's blood and takes Faith's dagger from the weapons chest. The Mayor devours the creatures from the Box of Gavroc, feeling stronger with each one he eats.

Buffy arrives at Faith's apartment and the fight takes them crashing through the window of Faith's apartment and onto a roof below. The fight moves inexorably to the edge of the roof and Buffy stabs Faith in the stomach with the Knife. Faith can't believe that Buffy's done it and falls back into a passing truck. Buffy rushes to the ledge, but she's too late. The truck, with Faith dead or unconscious, and the blood which Buffy needs to save Angel, is driving away…

## Graduation Day, Part Two (07/13/99), Episode:3ABB22

Written & Directed by Joss Whedon.

…Buffy escapes down the fire escape as Mayor Wilkins arrives. He is devastated by the thought of losing Faith and orders his vampires to find her. Xander and Giles are looking for information on the demon Olvikon. At the mansion, Buffy returns and feeds Angel the only Slayer's blood she can—her own. She falls unconscious from losing too much blood. Angel takes Buffy to the hospital and calls Giles and co to come to the hospital. A doctor talks to the Mayor as they stand around Faith in a hospital bed. The doctor explains that there's very little chance she'll ever regain consciousness.

Overhearing a nurse talk about another girl the Mayor quickly walks over to Buffy, and tries to suffocate her. Angel tears him away and the Mayor leaves, telling them not to miss the second act of the show. Giles and the gang show up at the hospital and Angel explains that Faith is in a coma, and that Buffy cured him when he drank her blood. Angel leaves, because the sun will be up soon and the rest go to check on Buffy. In her dreams, Buffy goes to Faith's apartment where Faith is packing up her stuff. Faith tells Buffy that human weakness never goes away, not even his. Faith tells Buffy that it's time to go and then Buffy wakes up, walks over to Faith and kisses her forehead. Dressed, Buffy walks out to the waiting room, telling her friends to get everyone ready. Ready for war.

Buffy needs everyone's help, especially Xander because of his remembered military training (*Halloween*). The Mayor's weakness is Faith and she'll uses it. Wesley, heading back to England since Buffy left the organisation, turns up and offers to help in anyway he can. While Buffy explains her plan, the Mayor lays out his own plan... Buffy's plan involves creating a volcano substitute—a bomb.

At graduation the Mayor starts his speech, but the transformation starts before he expected it and after an eclipse, he becomes a 60-foot snake demon. As parents scatter, the students gather together in a large group and rip off their robes, revealing weapons and crosses, and initiate all out war against the demon. Fire launchers, crossbows are all employed. Principal Snyder is eaten by the snake demon. Cordelia kills a vampire, but Larry and Harmony get killed. Buffy taunts the demon with Faith's dagger, telling him how easily it slipped into her, and he chases her into the library. She jumps out the window, just as the Mayor notices it's full of explosives.

## Buffy Resources

### The World Wide Web:

Sites come and sites go, but you can get to the important ones from:

**The Buffy Episode Guide**
http://slayer.simplenet.com/tbcs/episodes/index.html

**The Complete Buffy Episode Guide**
http://www.buffyguide.com/

**The Slayer Fanfiction Archive**
http://www.slayerfanfic.com/index1.html

Loads of fan fiction about your favourite characters, this site is an act of love. This was until recently the home for AleXander's (he likes his name spelt like that) transcripts of the series. Tragically 20th Century Fox (always knowing how to bring new viewers into the fold) have make them take these down, which seems a little mean spirited; do they seriously think people are going to read these in preference to viewing the show or buying the videos? It wouldn't rankle so much if they could be bothered to release the videos either quickly or in the right order. But what the heck do I know? A tip of the hat from this writer, who incidentally has *all* the released videos, as well as tapes of the show.

Concerned people can write to 20th Century Fox to let them know your feelings in a polite fashion, care of Dennis L. Wilson, Keats McFarland & Wilson LLP, Penthouse Suite, 9720 Wilshire Blvd, Beverly Hills, CA 90212. Hey, perhaps they'll do the intelligent thing and get AleX to edit an official paperback release of the scripts...

### Books

Most of the below are authorised fiction about Buffy, the odd unauthorised book (like this one) is out there. I can't honestly say most of them are value for money - you're generally better off with *The Watchers Guide*, or searching out issues of *Cinefantastique*. Or wait for my gigantic book on Buffy...

*Buffy the Vampire Slayer - Gatekeeper 1: Out of the madness*, by Christopher Golden & Nancy Holder, Pocket Books, £4.99

*Buffy the Vampire Slayer - Gatekeeper 2: Ghost Roads*, by Christopher Golden & Nancy Holder, Pocket Books, £4.99

*Buffy the Vampire Slayer - Gatekeeper 3: Sons of Entropy*, by Christopher Golden & Nancy Holder, Pocket Books, £4.99

*Buffy the Vampire Slayer 1, Harvest*, by Richie Tankersley Cusick, Pocket Books £3.50

*Buffy the Vampire Slayer* 2: Halloween rain, by Christopher Golden & Nancy Holder, Pocket Books, £3.50

*Buffy the Vampire Slayer* 3: Coyote moon, by John Vornholt, Pocket Books, £3.50

*Buffy the Vampire Slayer* 4: Night of the living, by Arthur Byron, Pocket Books, £3.50

*Buffy the Vampire Slayer* 5: Blooded, by Christopher Golden, Pocket Books, £4.99

*Buffy the Vampire Slayer* 6: Child of the hunt, by Nancy Holder, Pocket Books, £4.99

*Buffy the Vampire Slayer (Movie Adaptation)*, by Richie Tankersley Cusick, Pocket Books £3.50

*Buffy the Vampire Slayer - The Xander years 1*, by Christopher Golden & Nancy Holder, Pocket Books, £4.99

*Buffy the Vampire Slayer: Obsidian Fate*, by Diana G. Gallagher, Pocket Books, £5.99

*Buffy the Vampire Slayer: The Official Sunnydale High Yearbook*, by Christopher Golden & Nancy Holder, Pocket Books, (Hardback) £9.99

*Buffy the Vampire Slayer: Return to Chaos*, by Craig Shaw Gardner, Pocket Books, £4.99

*Buffy the Vampire Slayer: The Watcher's Guide*, by Chris Golden & Nancy Holder, Pocket Books, £9.99

*Buffy Postcard Book*, Pocket Books, £5.99

*Buffy: Angel Chronicles I*, by Nancy Holder, Pocket Books, £4.99

*Buffy: Angel Chronicles II*, by Richie Tankersley Cusick, Pocket Books, £4.99

*Buffy: Angel Chronicles III*, by Nancy Holder, Pocket Books, £4.99

*Buffy: Immortal*, by Christopher Golden & Nancy Holder, Pocket Books, (Hardback), £12.99

*Buffy: Power of Persuasion*, by Elizabeth Massie, Pocket Books, £4.99

*Buffy: Resurrecting Ravana*, by Ray Garton, Pocket Books, £4.99

*Buffy: Sins of the Father*, by Christopher Golden, Pocket Books, £5.99

*Buffy: Unnatural Selection*, by Mel Odom, Pocket Books, £4.99

*Buffy: Visitors*, by Laura Anne Gilman & Josepha Sherman, Pocket Books, £4.99

*Meet the Stars of Buffy the Vampire Slayer*, by Jan Gabriel, Scholastic, £3.99

*Buffy, the Vampire Slayer Exposed*, by Nadine Crenshaw, Prima Publishing, £10.99

*Buffy the Vampire Slayer 1: The Dust Waltz* (Graphic Novel), by Dan Brereton & Hector Gomez, Titan Books, £6.99

*Buffy the Vampire Slayer 2: The Remaining Sunlight*(Graphic Novel), by Andi Watson & Joe Bennett, Titan Books, £7.99

*Buffy the Vampire Slayer: The Origin*, by Dan Bereton, Chris Golden, Joe Bennett & Rick Ketcham(Graphic Novel), Titan Books, £7.99

*Buffy Chronicles*, by N E Genge, Three Rivers Press, £9.99

## Videos

In September the first two *Buffy* videos hit the stores, intelligently presenting *Welcome To The Hellmouth/The Harvest* and *Surprise/Innocence*. And you thought we needed television companies to show episodes out of order. Oh well, at least they won't be cut.

## Comics and Magazines

Titan start producing the Buffy magazine in the UK from September 1999, and Dark Horse have an ever expanding line of Buffy comics, only available from specialist shops - Forbidden Planet, etc. You can contact Forbidden Planet for mail order at 71 New Oxford Street, London, WC1A 1DG. tel:+44 71 497 2150

## Toys

Nah, not really, although there are some limited edition statues. You need to check out Forbidden Planet or similar venue.